# The Tempest

D1355432

## ARDEN STUDENT SKILLS: LANGUAGE AND WRITING

*Series Editor:*
Dympna Callaghan
Syracuse University

**Published Titles**
*The Tempest: Language and Writing*, Brinda Charry

**Forthcoming Titles**
*Macbeth*, Emma Smith
*Hamlet*, Dympna Callaghan
*Othello*, Laurie Maguire
*Twelfth Night*, Frances E. Dolan
*Romeo and Juliet*, Catherine Belsey
*King Lear*, Jean Howard
*A Midsummer Night's Dream*, Heidi Brayman Hackel

# The Tempest

Language and Writing

## BRINDA CHARRY

B L O O M S B U R Y

LONDON • NEW DELHI • NEW YORK • SYDNEY

**Bloomsbury Arden Shakespeare**

An imprint of Bloomsbury Publishing Plc

| | |
|---|---|
| 50 Bedford Square | 175 Fifth Avenue |
| London | New York |
| WC1B 3DP | NY 10010 |
| UK | USA |

**www.bloomsbury.com**

First published 2013

**British Library Cataloguing-in-Publication Data**
A catalogue record for this book is available from the British Library.

ISBN: HB: 978-1-4725-1827-9
PB: 978-1-4081-5289-8
ePDF: 978-1-4081-9042-5
ePub: 978-1-4081-5602-5

**Library of Congress Cataloging-in-Publication Data**
A catalogue record for this book is available from the British Library.

Typeset by Newgen Imaging Systems Pvt Ltd, Chennai, India
Printed and bound in India

# CONTENTS

# SERIES EDITOR'S PREFACE

This series puts the pedagogical expertise of distinguished literary critics at the disposal of students embarking upon Shakespeare Studies at university. While they demonstrate a variety of approaches to the plays, all the contributors to the series share a deep commitment to teaching and a wealth of knowledge about the culture and history of Shakespeare's England. The approach of each of the volumes is direct yet intellectually sophisticated and tackles the challenges Shakespeare presents. These volumes do not provide a shortcut to Shakespeare's works but instead offer a careful explication of them directed towards students' own processing and interpretation of the plays and poems.

Students' needs in relation to Shakespeare revolve overwhelmingly around language, and Shakespeare's language is what most distinguishes him from his rivals and collaborators – as well as what most embeds him in his own historical moment. The *Language and Writing* series understands language as the very heart of Shakespeare's literary achievement rather than as an obstacle to be circumvented. This series addresses the difficulties often encountered in reading Shakespeare alongside the necessity of writing papers for university examinations and course assessment. The primary objective here is to foster rigorous critical engagement with the texts by helping students develop their own critical writing skills. *Language and Writing* titles demonstrate how to develop students' own capacity to articulate and enlarge upon their experience of encountering the text, far beyond summarizing, paraphrasing or 'translating' Shakespeare's language into a more palatable, contemporary form. Each of the volumes in the series introduces the text as an act of specifically literary language and shows that the multifarious issues of life and history that Shakespeare's work addresses cannot be separated from their expression in language. In addition, each book takes students through a series of guidelines about how to develop viable undergraduate critical essays on the text in question, not by delivering interpretations, but rather by taking readers step-by-step through the process of discovering and developing their own critical ideas.

All the books include chapters examining the text from the point of view of its composition, that is, from the perspective of Shakespeare's own process of composition as a reader, thinker and writer. The opening chapters consider when and how the play was written, addressing, for example, the extant literary and cultural acts of language from which Shakespeare constructed his work – including his sources – as well as the generic, literary and theatrical conventions at his disposal. Subsequent sections demonstrate how to engage in detailed examination and analysis of the text and focus on the literary, technical and historical intricacies of Shakespeare's verse and prose. Each volume also includes some discussion of performance. Other chapters cover textual issues as well as the interpretation of the extant texts for any given play on stage and screen, treating, for example, the use of stage directions or parts of the play that are typically cut in performance. Authors also address issues of stage/film history as they relate to the cultural evolution of Shakespeare's words. In addition, these chapters deal with the critical reception of the work, particularly the newer theoretical and historicist approaches that have revolutionized our understanding of Shakespeare's language over the past 40 years. Crucially, every chapter contains a section on 'Writing matters', which links the analysis of Shakespeare's language with students' own critical writing.

The series empowers students to read and write about Shakespeare with scholarly confidence and hopes to inspire their enthusiasm for doing so. The authors in this series have been selected because they combine scholarly distinction with outstanding teaching skills. Each book exposes the reader to an eminent scholar's teaching in action and expresses a vocational commitment to making Shakespeare accessible to a new generation of student readers.

Professor Dympna Callaghan
Series Editor
*Arden Student Skills: Language and Writing*

# PREFACE

William Shakespeare's *The Tempest* is among the best-known and widely-admired works of literature. It has also been subject to energetic critical debate and lent itself more than any Shakespeare play to rewriting and appropriation. It is among the most 'metadramatic' of Shakespeare's plays, pondering the meaning and value of creating worlds with words. Written for the public stage, the play is also infused by the awareness that language is 'discourse' – a social event determined by and shaping social relationships. This book studies the language of the play both in appreciation of it and to demonstrate that form and content are integrated in this unique piece of literature that is as beautiful as it is profound.

The Introduction raises questions regarding literary language with specific reference to *The Tempest*. Can the play be appreciated as a thing of beauty even as one engages with its complex and sometimes disturbing philosophical and political themes? What is the relation between form and content? This introductory chapter also attempts to get readers to see literary language in all its material density: so the play's date of composition and the occasion for the first performance not only influenced the author's style but also resulted in a marked self-consciousness about language in the theatre. This section further discusses the play's genre as an aspect of its style, and evokes the formalist idea of the 'defamiliarizing' function of literature in order to look for connections between 'theme' and 'language' and between 'form' and 'content'. The 'Writing matters' section approaches the meaning and value of critical reading and writing, and prompts students to reflect on how first responses to the play (on the one hand, an instinctive appreciation of its beauty and complexity, or, on the other hand, the nervousness caused by its perceived difficulty) can constitute the basis of a critical engagement with the text.

Chapter 1 ('Language in print') examines how the print history of the play has impacted its style and also analyses how the play negotiates both the poetic and the communicative function of language. The analysis employs the concepts of narrative dialogism, linguistic ambiguity and paradox to examine key passages. This complicates our understanding of the central characters (specifically Prospero, Caliban and Miranda) and also our response to what constitutes the play's moral and ideological systems. The 'Writing matters' section explains how explication and close reading are the basis of any critical analysis and provides students prompts to exercise their close-reading skills and to move close reading toward critical analysis.

*The Tempest*, like other literary texts, is characterized by internal patterning or the deliberate arrangement of sound, diction and syntax and the manipulation of language in figurative speech. Chapter 2 ('Language: Forms and uses') is an examination of these formal patterns and techniques. It addresses how meaning is made in spite of or because of the slippery nature of figurative speech. The play's use of humour, and other kinds of rhetoric (praying, cursing and the language of courtship) are also addressed here. Imagery and symbolism are discussed as instances of the combination of the particular and concrete object or entity with the universal and abstract idea and experience. This chapter explores other 'special effects' – the use of music, the structure and purpose of the embedded masque, as well as the numerous intertextual relations by way of allusions and quotations that make up the discursive fabric of the play. The 'Writing matters' section includes questions and exercises that will get students to analyse each of these stylistic devices and techniques to greater extent.

Literary language is an instance of language as public discourse in that there is no immediate personal relation between the writer and the listener or the reader, and the text can be read or performed later in time and place in unprecedented contexts to unknown audiences. Chapter 3 ('Language through time') introduces readers to the critical and performance history (stage and film) of the play to demonstrate how the language of the play has provoked a range of interpretations. The notions of dialogism and intertextuality are evoked once more to study the literary appropriations of *The Tempest* and the ways in which they refresh our understanding and appreciation of the original text. The writing exercises for this chapter mainly focus on getting readers to consider questions of critical methodology, that is, how and why we read in certain ways. It is hoped that the questions here will help students become more aware of the assumptions informing different critical readings and more deliberate in their own critical engagement with the play.

While Chapter 4 ('Writing and language skills') touches on the examination response and offers ideas for online writing exercises, its main focus is the critical analysis paper. It offers tips on identifying a topic, arriving at a thesis and assembling evidence to back up the latter. It also explores the meaning, method and purpose of conducting research, including online research, on the play, and, finally, on the writing and organization of a critical paper. The chapter is followed by a list of book and article titles and online sources that may be consulted by those who wish to do further reading on the play.

# Introduction

In the fourth act of William Shakespeare's play *The Tempest*, the spirit Ariel, who is helping Prospero orchestrate the play towards its conclusion, reports that he has successfully charmed Caliban and his newfound friends, Trinculo and Stephano, who were by then 'red-hot with drinking' (4.1.171). At the sound of his tabor, Ariel says, 'like unbacked colts they pricked their ears, / Advanced their eyelids, lifted up their noses / As they smelt music; so I charmed their ears' (4.1.176–8). Ariel's music is analogous to the language of the play itself, a language that is characterized by a concrete and sensuous particularity. Like Caliban and his companions who respond immediately and absolutely to the music, readers of *The Tempest* too are continually enchanted by the language of the play. We too respond 'calf-like'(4.1.179) and follow the paths that the music weaves across the landscape of the text, across 'lush and lusty' foliage (2.1.55), as well as 'toothed briars, sharp furzes, pricking gorse and thorns' (4.1.180), through the intricacies of plot, setting and character, and we gladly become immersed in this masterpiece of theatrical and literary illusion. And we too are not only immensely moved but also saddened and disturbed by this mysterious island that is 'full of noises' and by the happenings on it (3.2.135).

The enchanted island and its inhabitants, human, animal, fairy and monster, the wild waters of the opening storm, Prospero's anger and hostility towards his enemies, Gonzalo's loyalty, Antonio's ambitions, and, finally, the love that blossoms between the young Ferdinand and Miranda – all of these are remarkably immediate and vivid to the reader. Yet, they are ultimately creations of language. The language of

*The Tempest* is poetic language at its most lyrical and most lovely. At the same time, it carries a range of philosophical and political meanings, which are as troubling and difficult to decipher as they are uplifting. How does the play function as both a thing of beauty and a vehicle for thought? Similar to Ariel's music, is enchantment the dominant effect of the play? In other words, does the language invite responses that are ultimately emotional and appreciative? Or, does it work to 'alienate' readers and audiences in the Brechtian sense, making it possible for us to step away from its beauty and to resist the magic, in order to think? In other words, can all poetry, including that of *The Tempest*, be philosophical and ideological as well as poetic? These are questions we grapple with as we engage with this play that is as beautiful as it is complex and recognize that both the beauty and complexity are effects of the linguistic prowess of the writer who an admiring contemporary described as the 'mellifluous and hony-tongued *Shakespeare*'.

The date of the play's original composition has bearing on its language. Although the date of composition is notoriously difficult to determine in the case of Renaissance drama as plays were written as theatrical scripts and went through multiple revisions and rewritings even before they were published, *The Tempest* is often regarded as Shakespeare's last play. By the nineteenth century, scholars were of the opinion that they had established the chronological order of the plays and determined that *The Tempest* was written shortly before the author's retirement to his birthplace and only a few years before his death in 1616. The earliest recorded performance of the play was at the royal court, on 'Hallomas Nyght', 1 November 1611. In the year 1603, Shakespeare's acting company had acquired the patronage of King James and became known as the King's Company or the King's Men. It was this company that 'presented att Whithall before the kings Majestie a play Called the Tempest'. Although, as it turns out, *Henry VIII* was written two years after *The Tempest*, as was the collaborative play *The Two Noble Kinsmen*, it can be said that Shakespeare, while writing it, intended *The Tempest* to be his farewell to the theatre. The playwright's literary technique and versification quite inevitably developed and changed through his career, and the play is in many ways the culmination of his experience in writing poetic drama. In the language of this play, we see some of the exquisite lightness of touch that marks the earlier comedies such as *As You Like It* and *Twelfth Night*, the vivid imagery and striking figurative language that prompted later poets like T. S. Eliot to admire the intensity of tragedies such as *Macbeth*, as well as the abstract and somewhat ponderous rhetoric of *Hamlet*. This is accompanied by a marked self-consciousness on the part of the author regarding the meaning and function of poetic language. On the one hand, he is aware that human thoughts become manifest only through language and that being itself reaches completion in and through it. As Miranda tells Caliban, 'I endowed thy purposes / With words that made them known' (1.2.358–59). 'Purposes' and 'words' are inextricably interwoven; without the proper expression, however elevated the purpose, one merely gabbles 'like / A thing most brutish' (1.2.357–8). Moreover, in this last play, Shakespeare is also clearly aware of language as discourse, that is, as meaning made in material conditions, shaped and reshaped by context and the relations between speaker and addressee. This is why Caliban can appropriate Prospero's language, remake that language and eventually use it to curse. Shakespeare also, however, ponders the enduring value of making meaning and creating worlds through language. In *Macbeth* too, he wondered if all tales are instances of idiotic blabbering, if words, in spite of their 'sound and fury', are ultimately meaningless, 'signifying nothing' (5.5.27–8), and in *Hamlet*, the young prince contemplates the futility of 'words, words, words' (2.2.192). Finally, in *The Tempest*, Shakespeare wonders if there is enduring value to the 'baseless fabric' (4.1.151) of the magical worlds poetic language creates, even as the magic is all he has to call his own.

Shakespeare's early audience also impacted his language choices in significant ways. Stephen Orgel reminds us, 'A record of performance at court implies neither a play written for the court nor a first performance there.' So, while the play was most likely part of the public repertoire before the royal performance, it was performed again in 1613 as part of the festivities organized to celebrate the engagement of Princess Elizabeth to the Elector Palatine. The stylized language of the masque embedded in the play, the exotic locale evoked so vividly and the numerous songs were all probably a result of the court audience.

Traditionally, critics also viewed the language of *The Tempest* as manifesting the wisdom, peace and tranquillity of old age. The tendency was to identify Shakespeare with Prospero, to see Prospero's 'magick' as standing for Shakespeare's art. Like his magician-philosopher, Shakespeare too had, at the end of his life, it was suggested, reached a state of serenity and happy contemplation, a state reflected in the play's rhetoric of redemption and forgiveness. However, other readers have doubted the usefulness of this biographical reading. The play was, after all, produced in an era when collaborative writing was the norm rather than the exception, and besides, one should generally be wary of making simplistic connections between authors' lives and their work because the process by which 'life' translates into art is a complicated one. It follows then that the aura of peace, completion and serenity that one might sense at the conclusion of *The Tempest* (so Lytton Strachey writes) 'cannot be taken as evidence of serene tranquillity on the part of their maker; they merely show that he knew, as well as anyone else, how such stories ought to end'.

Whether *The Tempest* was truly the last play or not, whether it was intended for royalty or not, what we can infer with some certainty is that it was a popular play in its time. Even the fact that Shakespeare's rival playwright Ben Jonson mentions it in his own work *Bartholomew Fair* (1614) indicates that *The Tempest* was well known (though Jonson himself clearly did not have – or would not admit to – any special regard for it). Besides, its position as the first play in the First Folio implies that it was a well-liked and admired piece. And surely, it is a clever editorial decision to have the Folio with the spectacle invoked by the lines: *A tempestuous noise of thunder and lightning heard.*

# The question of genre

Genre is admittedly a loose, perhaps even somewhat arbitrary, system of describing and classifying a literary text, but writers' consciousness of it has an impact on their language and other formal choices, just as genre sets up a framework of expectation for readers within which they respond to the work. Aristotle's *Poetics* defines tragedy and comedy as the two major genres in drama and describes them as formal categories with each having its own specific type of plot, structure and characterization. But genre can also be defined by the effect a literary work has on its audience and *also* by the world view or philosophy expressed in the text. Dramatic genre therefore means many things, and therefore, quite naturally, can sometimes mean very little. But this is not to imply that it can be dismissed in a study of the language of a text. As Russian Formalist critic Mikhail Bakhtin writes, 'Where there is style there is genre. The transfer of style from one genre to another not only alters the way a style sounds, under conditions of a genre unnatural to it, but also violates or renews the given genre.' Besides, because genres are categorized by style as well as by theme and content, genre is the space where the literary text as a self-contained artefact meets forces outside of itself, where 'purely' literary or formal aspects of a text encounter the historical and the contextual, or as Bakhtin writes, generic classifications are 'the drive belts from the history of society to the history of language'. Further, every literary text, by virtue of its generic affiliation, is characterized by a tension between the individual style and vision of the artist and the demands of a literary tradition that call for conformity and compliance. This tension has resulted in some of the most remarkable of literary works, including *The Tempest*.

The editors of the First Folio (this 1623 work is the first printed edition of Shakespeare's complete works) apparently did not have too many doubts about the genre that each of Shakespeare's plays belonged to and the title of this momentous work (*Mr. William Shakespeare's Comedies, Histories and Tragedies*) indicates that they felt that generic distinction did matter. *The Tempest* was quite simply classified under the 'Comedies' along with *Twelfth Night*, *As You Like It* and other plays whose place in this category continues to be unchallenged, and also along with *Measure or Measure* which has been designated as a 'problem play' or 'dark comedy'. *The Tempest* does exhibit some of the features of comedy. While nearly all of Aristotle's writings on comedy are lost to us, other treatises on the form do exist. Shakespeare would almost certainly have been introduced to the writings of the Roman writer Aelius Donatus (fourth century AD) in his grammar school Latin lessons, as well as the plays of the famous Latin comedy writer, Terence. Donatus explains that comedy is a sophisticated form, a product of civilizations in a higher state of development. It is concerned with real life but imitates stock literary types rather than distinct individual characters and is, above all, didactic. Many of these features are discernable in *The Tempest*. Ferdinand, Caliban and Gonzalo can be seen as character types of comedy (the brave young prince, the wild man, the loyal friend) and the play foregrounds the rhetoric of forgiveness and fidelity. Besides, the island setting with its lush landscape that is described in vivid detail is perhaps not all too different from the green world of *As You Like It* and much like the enchanted forest of *A Midsummer Night's Dream*, a world teeming with mystery, magic and spirits, good and bad. Like these other plays, *The Tempest* too ends on a note of reconciliation and harmony with the plot following the conventional comic trajectory from disorder to order. The protagonist is a lonely man in exile with his perhaps equally lonely daughter, but at the end of the narrative, the two of them find joy and community. Comedy after all takes its name from *komos*, the communal festivals celebrated by the ancient Greeks. *The Tempest* too concludes with reunions, hope and laughter. '[B]e cheerful / And think of each thing well' (5.1.250–1), Prospero advises his erstwhile enemies and promises them 'calm seas, auspicious gales / And sail so expeditious that shall catch / Your royal fleet far off' (5.1.315–18). The promised marriage at the end invokes the ancient fertility rituals in which all comedy had its origins. The young Ferdinand and Miranda will marry and continue the cycle of life. As for Caliban, even his villainy can be dismissed as clumsy and ludicrous, even rather clownish. Suffering, *real* suffering was experienced in the past, before the play even began.

But it is quite evident that many of these statements about the play's comic spirit can be challenged quite easily. The reader might be hard put to recognize in *The Tempest* the world of Shakespearean comedy, which Stanley Wells describes as 'unequalled in lyricism, in enjoyment of the spirit of laughter, in warmth of humour as well as sharpness of wit, in clear-sighted perception, understanding, and ultimately forgiveness of the waywardness of human behaviour'. Read in these terms, the play is perhaps not a comedy then, but a tragicomedy. Renaissance writers such as Philip Sidney might have disapproved of 'mongrel' plays that 'be neither right tragedies, nor right comedies, mingling kings and clowns' but Shakespeare and many of his contemporaries quite easily cast aside the niceties of genre and were comfortable with unruly but creative intermixtures. So, the comic spirit of *The Tempest* is informed by language that is tinged by sadness, anxiety and hopelessness. The world of the play is not quite as benign and joyous as that of the pastoral comedies. After all, the green woods have been inhabited by a witch who was horrifyingly deformed 'with age and envy' (1.2.258) and hapless spirits can be 'pegged' within the 'knotty entrails' of trees (1.2.295). While laughing at the ridiculous is an important feature of comedy, those who are rendered ridiculous by others (as Gonzalo is by Antonio and Sebastian, for example) are often kind and generous spirited. The jeering leaves us uncomfortable rather than delighted. And the 'clown' Caliban too is sometimes terrifying (as when he urges Stephano and Trinculo to inflict harm on Prospero, to 'Batter his skull, or paunch him with a stake, / Or cut his wezand with thy knife' (3.2.90–1)), often bitter, and sometimes very sad. The disappointments and antagonisms of tragedy are barely kept at bay.

But *The Tempest* is most often described as a romance. It was not until the nineteenth century that the play was so called, first by the Romantic poet Samuel Taylor Coleridge, but it is a designation that has persisted. The other Shakespeare plays usually included in the group are *Cymbeline*, *The Winter's Tale*, *Pericles* and *The Two Noble Kinsmen*. These four texts are a fairly diverse lot (*The Tempest* and *The Winter's Tale* appear as comedies in the Folio, and *Cymbeline* is classified under the tragedies. *Pericles* and *The Two Noble Kinsmen* do not appear in the Folio), but still hold some generic affinities. Broadly speaking, a romance is a fictitious narrative set in a distant time and place with events and characters far removed from the real. The writers of the European Middle Ages took up the genre enthusiastically to tell the stories of knightly adventures in distant lands. Though the Renaissance author George Puttenham mentions romances in *The Arte of English Poesie* (1589), he refers to them with some condescension as 'stories of old time'. But Shakespeare looks at the past, into what Prospero describes the 'backward and abysm of time' (1.2.50) and finds fresh material.

Like the conventional romance, the island setting right away distances *The Tempest* from the everyday realities of life. This is a separate world governed by its own energies and rhythms, a world in which spirits that 'make midnight-mushrooms' (5.1.39) and playfully chase the waves 'on the sands with printless foot' (5.1.34) are real, as is a hooped witch and her 'hag-born' (1.2.282) monster child. The characters too are transformed by the awareness that they have been transported to another level of existence. As Alonso says, 'These are not natural events; they strengthen / From strange to stranger'

(5.1.227–8). Besides, in *The Tempest*, one can discern traces of the tale of the Virgilian hero Aeneas who is perhaps the first of the romance heroes (although the *Aeneid* is doubtless an epic), and who is also, like Prospero, an unwilling exile and voyager. And, like Aeneas, it is Prospero's awareness of his child's right to life, and later to royal status and power that motivates him to act. When he tells Miranda that 'Thou wast that did preserve me' (1.2.153), the line is among the most simple and tender ones that he utters and also the most telling. The basic structure of the adventure story – the departure, the quest, the discovery, the conflict and the return, all fundamental to the romance genre – is enacted in the play. Unlike other Shakespearean plays, the story of *The Tempest* is an original one (as far as we know), but the playwright draws upon Renaissance accounts of travel to the 'New World', including narratives such as William Strachey's *True Repertory of the Wrack* and Sylvester Jourdain's *A Discovery of the Bermudas* (both ca. 1610), all of which are, in their own way, versions of the quest story. The language of *The Tempest* is thus a slightly odd but still fascinating blend of the romantic and the real, the marvellous and the historical. Like the poet whom Sidney exalts, Shakespeare is not tied down by the mundane and everyday. Instead, he is moved, in Sidney's words, by 'the vigour of his invention', and 'doth grow in effect into another nature: in making things better than nature bringeth forth, or quite anew, forms such as never were in nature'. But unlike Sidney's poet, he not only 'delivers a golden' world, but also marries it with the 'brazen'.

All four plays described as romances are stories of partings, loss and meetings. In all of them, high-born families are torn apart and reunite in faraway lands. There is none of the uproarious laughter of comedy in *The Tempest*, though the tragic themes of loss and parting are within the framework of the optimistic spirit of comedy. Indeed, even the most traumatic of Prospero's experiences has occurred before he reached the island and the edge of his pain has perhaps dulled. The play is relatively untouched by the terror and agony of the tragic vision, and its conclusion is instead informed (for most of the characters) by hope and by reconciliation with oneself and others, though both the hope and reconciliation have been hard earned. However, even as the play moves unswervingly towards its happy end, and even as Prospero says that it is best they do not 'burden our remembrances with / A heaviness that's gone' (5.1.199–200), the reader cannot help but be reminded, because of the presence of Caliban, because of Prospero's dark brooding thoughts and because of the presence of the villainous Antonio and Sebastian that the potential for tragedy always hovers over life's happiest moments, and that one man's happy ending might not be another's. The two main characters in the play, Prospero and his slave Caliban, are both lonely men and have been through some of the most intense experiences of their lives in solitude. It is a loneliness that neither of them, not even Prospero surrounded by friends and family in the last act, is able to quite shed. And though home waits at the end of the final journey, after that, always, comes death. As Prospero says, 'Every third thought shall be my grave' (5.1.312). Thus, Shakespeare takes up and transforms the romance, making the adventure a narrative of the journey through life and creating monsters and enemies that lurk both without and within the self.

*The Tempest* also borrows heavily from yet another genre, the court masque. The masque was a popular court entertainment of the time in which actors as well as some of the nobility in court dressed in ornate costumes and against lavish artificial backdrops performed little skits with lyrical dialogues and dances, but skimpy plots and little or no characterization. The masque was especially popular in the court of King James, encouraged by his wife Queen Anne. Shakespeare's rival Ben Jonson provided the script for many well-known masques, though somewhat surprisingly Shakespeare was never directly involved in the writing of one. The masque is best understood within the context of Jacobean court culture and pageantry. Some scholars would argue that the King's Men company's acquisition of the more upmarket indoors

Blackfriars theatre in 1608 is an event that had a great deal to do with the kind of play *The Tempest* is. The indoors theatre afforded the playwright the ornate settings that the Globe did not. While, as mentioned earlier, too much should perhaps not be made of the Blackfriars stagings, because *The Tempest* might have been enacted at both the Globe and the Blackfriars, it is still true that some of the scenes in the play that are characterized by stylized poetic language, such as the pageant in Act 4 involving Ceres and the other goddesses to celebrate the betrothal of Ferdinand and Miranda, are clearly brief masques embedded within the play. *The Tempest* also has more songs and instrumental pieces than any of Shakespeare's other plays (Ben Jonson in fact takes a sly dig at the play in his *Bartholomew Fair* when he makes fun of 'those that beget Tales, Tempests, and such-like drolleries'). The music does not simply constitute charming little interludes, but also plays an important role in the plot. The 'sweet airs' (3.2.136) of the island lure Ferdinand to Miranda, put the nobles to sleep and get Caliban and his conspirators into trouble.

It is not just the lavishness of song, dance and spectacle that is significant about the Jacobean court masque. The pageantry itself was a celebration of the power and glory of the monarch and the grandeur of the royal court. Conversely, the monarch's power was reinforced by the spectacle. It is significant that Prospero, with the help of Ariel, conjures up the masque with Ceres and the other mythological figures at a time when he begins to feel more confident of his control over his erstwhile enemies. 'Go bring the rabble', he commands Ariel (4.1.37); he wants to impress them with the 'vanity of mine art' (4.1.41), his ability to conjure up brilliant worlds of power and wonder, as well as to draw them – now that he has forgiven them – into the circle of his beneficent authority. 'No tongue, all eyes. Be silent!' he orders (4.1.59), and the masque begins. The 'rabble' are only spectators but their act of viewing is important for Prospero to establish his glory and power. The Jacobean masque had great political import and was ultimately a tribute to the wise and benevolent ruler who restores order, much like Prospero does by the end of the play. Many masques also incorporated in their structures farcical little interludes known as antimasques with grotesque, unruly characters. If we want to read *The Tempest* as an extended masque, Caliban can perhaps be seen as an element of the antimasque. He is disruptive, but only temporarily so, and ultimately, he too becomes part of the prevailing order.

However, as with the other generic classifications, one has to be careful about calling *The Tempest* a masque, even a modified one. After all, the complex plot and five-act structure are far more elaborate than that of any masque. Besides, masques were unambiguous in their celebration of the king and there was a straightforwardness and clarity to their political purpose. Prospero's masque, however, ends abruptly and in chaos when the nymphs and reapers 'heavily vanish' 'to a strange, hollow, and confused noise' (4.1). This is not quite a vision of order. Prospero's power may not be unambiguously celebrated in the play, and neither is Caliban simply the unruly wild man of the antimasque.

In addition to these categories, *The Tempest* has been read as a religious allegory, much in the tradition of medieval mystery and morality plays, by those who would argue that the ultimate message of the play is a moral, specifically Christian, one, and that reconciliation, restoration and the hope of divine redemption are central to the narrative. It also has been described as a narrative in the pastoral tradition because of its bucolic setting, and because it sets the ideal world of nature against the corruption of the court and other man-made institutions. It has further been seen as having affinities to other Renaissance narratives of utopia, with the island becoming the space where an ideal commonwealth is possible. But it is quite obvious that no single category can simply be applied to the play. This is true of many literary texts. As Lawrence Danson writes, genres do not exist 'as unchanging essences but as sets of loose similarities among artworks widely separated in their historical and cultural assumptions'. As readers, we use a text's genre not only to recognize its affinity to other works, but also to see its difference. The *idea* of genre, as Danson puts it, is 'never equal to the shifting reality of actual theatrical or literary practice'. The play is the result of Shakespeare's exploration and creative revision, even perhaps subversion, of diverse literary traditions and therefore has a role in their making and dynamic continuation. So, *The Tempest* is a wonderfully indeterminable species of play. 'What have here', Trinculo asks in drunken befuddlement when he stumbles upon Caliban, 'a man or a fish?' (2.2.24–5). We too are not quite sure what we have with *The Tempest*, but its ambiguous genre gives the language of the play a variety and richness of tone and meaning that is unusual even for a Shakespeare play.

# Theme

'Now it is tyme to speake of the matter or subject of Poesie', writes Shakespeare's contemporary George Puttenham after painstakingly defending the merit and importance of poetry. As far as Puttenham is concerned, 'whatsoever wittie and delicate conceit of man meet or worthy to be put in written verse, for any necessary use of the present time, or good instruction of posteritie' is a fit subject for writing. He goes on to explain that literary themes should be directed towards celebrating God, or earthly Princes, and, in general, should inspire, console and entertain mankind. Sidney too writes that poetry is particularly suited to these tasks. The 'feigned image of poetry' in fact 'instructs and delights' in a manner superior to philosophy that deals with the 'abstract and the general', and history that deals only with the particular. It is the literary alone that combines the 'the general notions with the particular example'.

These 'general notions' expressed in a literary text, its central preoccupations, its 'subject matter', the statements it makes about life, the self and the world, constitute its theme or themes and are usually of interest to critics and readers. The theme of a story might or might not be what inspires a writer, and it is hard to tell (certainly in the case of Shakespeare) the extent to which writers are conscious of executing a theme in their work. It is, therefore, more productive to avoid committing the 'intentional fallacy' or trying to speculate on the author's intended meaning and to think instead about the relationship between a text's thematic concerns and its language. It is arguably true of all instances of human communication, but especially true of literary texts, that neither do ideas simply lie behind language, nor is language a mirror reflecting ideas and entities outside of itself; on the other hand, language is constitutive of content. Form and content are inseparable in literature and one cannot comment on one without taking the other into consideration. The enterprise of criticism is precisely this – to make connections between what is being said and how it is said. Meaning is made by diction, syntax, structure and sound, and it is impossible to ignore these elements of the text (that *are* the text, in fact) and focus on distilling its 'meaning' alone. However, Terry Eagleton also warns against what he calls 'the mimetic theory of form' or the insistence on seeing form as imitative of content, the need to see all literary language as onomatopoeic in some sense, and sound as echoing sense in some simplistic way. In Eagleton's words, 'Grasping the "what" of content in terms of the "how" of form, however, does not necessarily mean seeing the two as harmoniously united . . . form and content can be at loggerheads. . . . Indeed, it is fortunate that they can be, since otherwise a whole range of fascinating poetic effects would be ruled out. These are the kind of effects one gets from playing the one off against the other, setting up tensions and ambiguities between the two.'

These reflections on language, form and theme are useful as one approaches the themes of *The Tempest*. The play's generic complexity and the richness and variety of its language not only make it difficult to pin down a single theme, but also make it possible to examine how language and form constitute and relate to the text's thematic concerns. For instance, the play's lyrical language and fantasy narrative is at odds with what can be read as its central theme: political struggle and the problems of dynastic succession, topics of interest to King James who wrote extensively on these issues. Prospero's political problems begin when he 'to my state grew stranger' (1.2.76). Eventually, another power struggle between Prospero and Caliban dominates. The relationship between the magus and his slave has been read as the relationship between colonizer and colonized, especially in the context of the European settlement of the Americas (also a topic of great interest to both King James and his son, Prince Henry). Race and colonial relations, political and cultural hegemony contribute to the play's central conflicts. It is from the tension between the enchanting language on the one hand and the hard-headed nature of political drama (and the play has all the makings of the latter with false brothers, treacherous allies, rebellious slaves and young heirs deprived of their political legacy) on the other, that a discussion of this particular aspect of the play's content can emerge. Along the same lines, Shakespeare also reminds us that politics is ultimately a human enterprise. So, the play is also a story about human frailties and human goodness, our propensity for anger, resentment and the desire for revenge, as well as the ability and even need to forgive. The formal trajectory of the play is characterized by the movement from anger to forgiveness and reconciliation. The rhetoric of forgiveness and community inform the conclusion. One may ask how this can be reconciled with the cloak and dagger world of political wheeling and dealing.

It could be argued however, that form is a reflection of content when it comes to another aspect of the play: magic. Both Prospero and Sycorax are magicians. The figure of the powerful magus preoccupied Renaissance writers and they used it to explore the meaning and end of human aspiration. Male versus female, good versus bad knowledge, white versus black are some of the binaries along which the language of the play is constructed. However, a careful reading of structure could well lead to the recognition that the play deconstructs rather than reinforces these opposites, thus leading to a more complex understanding of the theme of magic.

Formalist critics would argue that language itself is the theme of literature, that all literature is self-referential in the final analysis. *The Tempest* is without doubt also about quite another kind of magic, the power of language and art to create and dismantle reality. The play clearly ends with a vision of the staged spectacle of theatre: 'The cloud-capped towers, the gorgeous palaces, / The solemn temples, the great globe itself' (4.1.152–3). Indeed, this aspect of *The Tempest* has fascinated writers and artists across the ages and the English Romantic poets of the nineteenth century, who were preoccupied with the meaning and role of art and the imagination in shaping experience, often spoke of their achievements in terms of Prospero's magic. It can therefore be said that *The Tempest* is the most metapoetic of Shakespeare's plays and quite self-consciously reflects on the wondrous business of making art, especially drama, the lessons art teaches, the relationship between art and religion and art and reality.

For other readers, the play is quite simply about Shakespeare himself. This kind of reading presupposes that language is fundamentally a revelation of the self, the utterance cannot be distinguished from the speaker, and in the case of literature, the person, the artist and the text are intertwined. As discussed earlier, *The Tempest* has been often read as a semi-autobiographical work. Shakespeare was first identified with Prospero in 1838 though the association had already been established in the 1700s when a statue of the poet was erected in Westminster Abbey with an inscription from Prospero's famous 'our revels are now ended' speech (4.1.148–163). The fact that *The Tempest* is among Shakespeare's last plays has encouraged readers to read it as a key to the playwright's personality and his reflections on his career, success, age and impending death. The nineteenth-century scholar Edward Dowden wrote that we associate Prospero with his creator because of his 'harmonious and fully developed will'. Prospero, Dowden believed, reveals not only Shakespeare's faults (impatience, short temper) but also his 'abiding strength and self-possession'. The artist Shakespeare and the man Shakespeare are then, for critics such as Dowden, quite simply, the themes of *The Tempest*.

A number of other themes can be listed: the play is about father–child relations. Hence, Alonso is a broken man when he thinks he has lost his son, and Prospero's most prized possession is his daughter. The structure of the play depends on the tension between the old and the young, as well as each one's dependence on the other. Similarly, the language of the play explores the range of feelings children have for their fathers with Ferdinand's mourning his supposedly dead parent accompanied by hauntingly beautiful song, and Miranda's using a remarkable variety of tones with Prospero – she admires, pleads with, fears and sometimes simply tolerates her aging father. In fact, it can be said that the father–daughter relationship lies at the centre of this and many other Shakespeare's plays. After all, the Renaissance father is the first representative (and in the case of Miranda practically the only representative) of the patriarchal order as far as the woman of the time period is concerned, and exploring the father–daughter relationship in this play gives us occasion to explore gender roles and gender relations as a prominent thematic concern. Like that other aging parent, King Lear, Prospero too places great weight on the recognition and status that go with his position as a patriarch.

Even this brief outline of the themes of *The Tempest* makes it quite clear that the concerns of the play are so numerous and so varied that the reader is hard put to reconcile or to look for valid connections between them. The point is that it is difficult to simply 'summarize' the themes of a good literary text. That would, in fact, defeat the purpose of the text itself. Even if one is unwilling to fully subscribe to the poet Archibald MacLeish's statement that 'Poetry should not mean / but be', one will concede that a literary work is neither merely a vehicle for meaning, nor could the 'meaning' conceivably exist without language. What a good piece of art, like *The Tempest*, does is, to adopt another Russian formalist critic Viktor

Shklovsky's term, 'defamiliarize' both language and content. Shklovsky writes that our perception of the word gradually becomes habituated and automated; we don't really sense things or know ideas and thoughts in their uniqueness after a while. This is reflected in our use of language – we leave sentences unfinished and resort to the same tired phrases repeatedly. We take both language and the world for granted. What art does, says Shklovsky, is 'impart the sensation of things as they are perceived and not as they are known. The technique of art is to make objects "unfamiliar" to make forms difficult, to increase the difficulty and length of perception'. Poetic language, is itself a defamiliarization of everyday language, and daily speech rendered strange and beautiful serves to 'remove the automatic nature of perception'. This theorization of the function of art serves well to understand the workings of language in relation to the content of *The Tempest*. The language of the play forces us to look closely at it. It is not simply a medium for expression, it is opaque, an entity that needs to be perceived for itself. It thus defamiliarizes our worn out everyday discourse. In doing so, it also leads us to look at its content – whether that be power, colonial relations, magic or gender – in new ways. Like all good literature, it refreshes our experience of language and in doing so renews our perception of the world and its ways.

## Writing matters

*The Tempest* is read for a number of reasons – for pleasure, because it is a famous play written by a famous author, in order to get ready to play one of the characters in the play, or because it has been assigned to a class. Whatever the reason, it is necessary to train oneself as a critical reader. To read critically implies a deep and active engagement with the text in order to understand it better. Critical reading is not entirely distinct from 'reading for enjoyment'. It is intellectually invigorating and leads to a deeper involvement with and appreciation of the literary text. It is from such a close and dynamic engagement with a text that critical writing emerges. It involves asking good questions about the play, identifying topics to write about, constructing an argument that is worthwhile and interesting and writing a critical response that might vary in length from a short paragraph to a longer essay. A critical response is not only a stimulating writing exercise but it is actually also a good reading exercise because it compels us to look more closely at the play. It enhances the reading experience by alerting us to aspects of the language that we might otherwise notice only vaguely in passing. It also makes us appreciate some of the skill and effort that has gone into writing the play.

A critical response is a result of thought and meditation but is still shaped by our initial responses to the play. We first *experience* a literary text rather than process it critically. These earliest responses are important and valuable and the questions and writing exercises in this section are ways of allowing you to integrate your initial experience of the text into your critical analysis of it.

1 One of the obvious reasons one reads is for pleasure. Pleasure might come from a text's aesthetic dimensions (its ingenious use of language, the story, the structure of the piece), it might also come from the fact that the narrative 'speaks' to us in some ways – perhaps we think the story has a moral theme or ideological agenda that is particularly appealing to us. Reflect briefly on kind of enjoyment reading *The Tempest* yields for you. Consider whether the poetic and political, the poetic and the moral, even the moral and political elements of the play are at odds with each other. Finally, think about the connections between simply 'experiencing' a literary text and 'analysing' it, and the process by which experience/enjoyment becomes analysis.

2 In Chapter 1, we will touch on the differences between reading a play and other forms of fictional

narrative such as the novel or the short story, but the inescapable fact that *The Tempest* is a play most likely has an impact on our experience and understanding of the text. A play has no narrator – the story is not presented to us through a single dominant consciousness. Discuss whether this results in the reader being unable to identify or empathize with any single character and whether this manner of identification is necessary to truly immerse oneself in and derive pleasure from a text.

**3** The language of *The Tempest* might pose some difficulties. Reflect on what exactly we mean by the 'difficulty' of a literary text. Is it to do with the organization of the story or the obscurity of the language? Consider whether the fact that *The Tempest* is not in contemporary English and the fact that it is drama (meant to be performed, rather than a novel, for example, that is meant only to be read) contributes to this difficulty. In our discussion above, we turned to the idea of literature as 'defamiliarizing' language. This implies that a play like *The Tempest* deviates from the linguistic norm. Reflect on the connections between the defamiliarizing function of literature and the difficulty it might pose to the reader.

**4** An unavoidable feature of *The Tempest* is that it is an older text. Our awareness of this profoundly impacts our experience of the play. The language of the play comes to us bearing the weight of a distant historical moment. This not only poses some obvious challenges to the reader, but also, perhaps, makes the text more intriguing. Discuss whether it is possible (and even better) to lift the text out of its historical moment, to divorce it of context and read it for its own sake, or whether an awareness of context is necessary both for enhanced enjoyment and sound literary analysis.

# CHAPTER ONE

# Language in print

The language of *The Tempest* is 'rich and strange' (1.2.402). It makes it possible and pleasurable for readers to suspend disbelief and to lose themselves in an enchanted realm of airy spirits, monsters, lost princes and storm-swept islands. For Philip Sidney, this is what the most elemental kind of poetry does; the poet, godlike, creates the 'might be and should be' rather than simply depicts what already is. For later poets like Coleridge the depiction of the fantastic was Shakespeare's major achievement in the play. Coleridge writes: '*The Tempest* is a specimen of the purely romantic drama, in which the interest is not historical, or dependent upon fidelity of portraiture, or the natural connection of events. . . . It addresses itself only to the imaginative faculty.' From this perspective, the play emerges from the inner life of the poet and provides the reader a feast of the imagination. Coleridge maintains that time, place and plot are secondary to this intended effect and the effect itself is achieved not only by the introduction of implausible elements into the narrative, but also by the author's use of words and images that barely have any reference points in the real. Ariel's song to Ferdinand who is wondering about his lost father is a good example of this:

> Full fathom five thy father lies,
> Of his bones are coral made;
> Those are pearls that were his eyes,
> Nothing of him that doth fade

But doth suffer a sea-change
Into something rich and strange.

                                        (1.2.397–402)

Even as the ditty is a song of mourning and reminds us of
the transformations that death brings about, the author's primary interest in these lines seems to be to revel in the lyrical and poetic for its own sake, to make vague and beautiful
connections between human bones and coral, unseeing eyes
and pearls, to aesthetically explore a richness and strangeness
that transcends human understanding, which indeed does
not really need to be understood, only experienced. There
are many such instances of language use in the play: when
Ferdinand swears with all the exuberance of the young lover
that '[t]he mistress which I serve quickens what's dead' (3.1.6),
when Ariel promises his master to 'divide/ And burn in many
places' (1.2.198–9) and later when he sings, 'Where the bee
sucks, there suck I' (5.1.88). All of these lines evoke a vague
mood that the reader can hardly name, but that never fails to
move. The beauty of language is what is foregrounded in such
lines; the mimetic function of language as a signifying system
and vehicle of communication appears to be secondary to its
poetic function. The language draws attention to, even flaunts
itself, and investigates its own potential and scope.

But oddly enough, *The Tempest* is also among the most
meaningful and profound of literary works. The themes outlined in the introductory chapter should give some indication
of the range of meanings that readers have noted, and demonstrate that the language of the play cannot be described
simply as self-referential and poetic. Even though Sebastian
describes Antonio's utterances as 'a sleepy language, . . .
thou speak'st / Out of thy sleep' (2.1.211–12), the regicide
and treachery they plot are real and urgent. Similarly, even
as Caliban's curses are characterized by hyperbole and draw
upon images from the fantastic ('As wicked dew as e'er my
mother brushed / With raven's feather from unwholesome fen
/ Drop on you both' (1.2.322–4)), the anger and hatred behind

his words are palpable and real, as is his claim: 'This island's mine by Sycorax, my mother, / Which thou tak'st from me' (1.2.332–3).

The language thus bears a range of philosophical, political and ideological meanings even as it is dreamlike and 'faery'. This combination of the real and earthy with the unreal and enchanted, and the sensuous and concrete with the elevated and abstract is among Shakespeare's major literary triumphs. Although generations of readers have been seduced by the loveliness of the poetry, they have also been moved to ask questions about what the play has to say and how it says it. And indeed the two are inseparable. Twentieth-century author Henry James notes that Shakespeare's writing illustrates 'the relation of style to meaning and of manner to motive'. *The Tempest* makes it clear that meaning cannot be separated from expression. This realization is crucial to both understanding and appreciating the play.

There is another dimension to *The Tempest* that one must be conscious of in order to fully appreciate it: the fact that it is drama. Unlike other forms of fictional narrative (the novel or short story, for instance), drama lacks the literary element of 'point of view'. There is neither a single dominant consciousness, nor is there a narrative voice to fill in details and provide commentary on the events and characters in the story. The reader must actively participate in fleshing out details of backdrop and character. Besides, since the narration is completely objective in that all the characters are invested with a voice and there is no narrator projecting any specific point of view, the reader must do the work of deciding which character offers the favoured perspective. Is *The Tempest* Prospero's story or is it Caliban's? In order to answer this and other questions, attention must be paid to the poetic as well as to the dramatic texture of a passage or scene. For example, even as one looks at the symbolism of the opening storm scene, one must also think about its dramatic significance and the work it does on stage for the audience of spectators. Like all of Shakespeare's plays, *The Tempest* is clearly a complex document: it is a piece of poetic language, it is a narrative that tells a story even as it conveys a range of meanings and it is also a dramatic script that is realized in performance.

## The play in print

Modern readers and actors inherit *The Tempest* in its printed form. Scholars who study the history of books as physical objects are of the opinion that examining the material form of books and the socio-economic circumstances from which they emerged is as important as analysing the language of a literary text for its effect and meaning. Indeed, they would argue, the two are connected.

Printing technology was fairly widespread but still quite expensive in Renaissance England and the fact that Shakespeare's works went into print fairly early on indicate that he was a reputed author. However, print also enhanced Shakespeare's stature and popularity. The quarto editions of several Shakespeare plays (though not of *The Tempest*) are still in existence. These quartos were probably prepared from the author's uncorrected manuscripts or from reconstructions of the play by members of the theatrical companies. Quartos might not have made Shakespeare much money but they helped build his reputation. By 1598, most quartos were published with Shakespeare's name prominently displayed on the title page. It has been argued by scholars that Shakespeare was a 'dual-mode' author who grasped the potential of the exciting new technology and produced texts with a view for both performance and publication. As historian of Renaissance printing and publishing practices, Andrew Pettegree, writes 'by embracing print he secured his place in the canon of literary greats even in his own time'.

Of course, to begin with, Shakespeare, like other playwrights of the period, would have written his first draft by hand in the 'secretary hand', which was the common script for the period. The 'bending author' (Epilogue 2) he mentions in his play *Henry V* would have laboured over his work wielding a hand-cut pen. Almost all our information on writing for the theatre and other theatrical practices in the time period comes from one Philip Henslowe, who was manager of the Rose Theatre and who maintained a fairly detailed record of the affairs of the theatre between 1590–2. While one cannot always extrapolate from Henslowe's account, one can make some inferences from it about the writing of *The Tempest*. Henslowe indicates that half to a two-thirds of the plays written at the time were collaborative efforts. Although we have no evidence of a co-author to *The Tempest*, actors, scriveners and printers have certainly had a role in shaping the play as we have inherited it. Like other playwrights, Shakespeare probably wrote *The Tempest* fairly speedily, in between four to six weeks, for an eager audience demanding new productions. The original drafts or 'foul papers' of the play would have been invaluable had they existed and made it possible for us to see how much Shakespeare revised the play as he went along. Shakespeare's colleagues from the King's Men and the editors of the First Folio, John Heminge and Henry Condell, maintained that Shakespeare was a natural genius to whom poetry came with little effort. None of the drudgery of revision and rewriting was for him for 'his mind and his hand went together. And what he thought, he uttered with that easiness, that we scarce received from him a blot in his papers'. The idea of Shakespeare's spontaneous talent has indeed been appealing, but revised versions of his work are intriguing in their own way. They not only help modern readers understand the creative process, but also emphasize that literary texts are unstable and indeterminate entities, even if the text in question is a Shakespeare play. In any case, the foul papers of *The Tempest* are lost to us, as are the prompt books that were prepared by theatrical companies; nor is the play available in a quarto edition. It appears for the first time in print in the First Folio.

The Folio, which is among the most important books in the world, was published by Heminge and Condell in 1623

(7 years after Shakespeare's death). The two men were inspired by their late friend's talent and popularity and motivated by the success of Ben Jonson's folio of his own collected works, published in 1616. Without the Folio, we wouldn't have had 18 plays – including *The Tempest* – none of which appeared previously in print as far as we know. The Folio also gave Shakespeare the status of the 'author' of his works in the modern sense. (The collaborative nature of playwriting and the fact that so much literary output in the time period was for the stage, meant that literary works were not always associated with a single authorial figure.) But the Folio prominently displayed Shakespeare's authorship of *The Tempest* and the 35 other plays in the collection. It was titled *Mr William Shakespeares Comedies, Histories, and Tragedies – published according to the True Original Copies* and prominently displayed the famous engraving of Shakespeare's head. About a thousand copies of the book (the maximum number allowed by the Stationer's Company) were produced of which 230 are still available. The plays were classified into genres as we have noted in the previous chapter and *The Tempest*, which heads the entire collection, is placed among the comedies.

It is not clear if *The Tempest* of the First Folio is the exact same play that was first performed on stage in 1611. In their preface, Heminge and Condell tell their 'great variety of readers' that earlier print versions of the plays were 'maimed and deformed by the frauds and stealths of injurious imposters'. What they offer, they claim, are 'cured and perfect versions'. This implies that the text of *The Tempest* as we have it was probably edited and revised post-performance. Besides, as Pettegree explains, 'The medium of print provided opportunities not available on the stage: to deepen character, to elaborate poetical, philosophical reflections that could be appreciated by the owner of the printed text.' Therefore, it looks like while the play *The Tempest* would not have come into existence without the vibrant and dynamic English Renaissance theatre, the literary text characterized by the complex and beautiful language that we read and enact today might not have come to be without the printing press.

The First Folio was so successful that a second edition was printed in 1632, a third in 1663–4 and a fourth in 1685. Thus, *The Tempest* was transmitted to readers for nearly half a century and it hasn't gone out of print since. Since there is only one version of the play, there are fewer textual issues that editors need to untangle. However, it is widely acknowledged that the First Folio was somewhat embellished by one Ralph Crane, a professional scrivener who produced the manuscript of the play in the 1620s, probably copied from Shakespeare's own draft or from a copy of it. It was to Crane's version that the editors of the First Folio turned. Crane re-punctuated texts, used elisions frequently ('cry o' h' sea', 'do'st', 'miss't' and 'in't', for example) and might have attempted to regularize metre. We also probably owe Crane the elaborate stage directions in the play including such samples as:

*Thunder and lightning. Enter Ariel, like a harpy, claps his wings upon the table, and with a quaint device the banquet vanishes.* (3.3)

and

*A noise of hunters heard. Enter diverse Spirits in shape of dogs and hounds, hunting them about, Prospero and Ariel setting them on.* (4.1)

These directions – sometimes almost novel-like in detail – were most likely based on version or versions of the play Crane watched. It is interesting to think about if and how they help the modern actor and how they alter the reader's experience of the text. Do they interrupt the narrative flow? Does the mention of the 'quaint device' (presumably some kind of stage machinery that is used to make the banquet vanish) take away from the magical experience?

Like all of the plays, editions of *The Tempest* too have changed over the centuries. In the eighteenth century, when editors thought nothing about interfering with a text to ensure that it met the literary and moral standards of the time, ambiguities and ambivalences in the language of the play were detected, classified as 'errors' and subject to correction. The 'perfect' text was valued more than the 'authentic' one. In the case of *The Tempest*, one particular change, for example, was made that alters readers' attitude to Miranda. In the second scene of Act 1, Miranda lashes out at Caliban:

> Abhorred slave,
> Which any print of goodness wilt not take,
> Being capable of all ill;

(1.2.352–4)

Starting with John Dryden and William Davenant in the seventeenth century, editors could not stomach the fact that the gentle Miranda could utter such harsh words, even if they were addressed to Caliban. These lines were therefore assigned to Prospero till the twentieth century when editors and readers were willing and able to view Miranda in more complex terms.

There is another interesting textual crux in *The Tempest*. After witnessing the spectacular masque in Act 4, Ferdinand exclaims:

> Let me live here ever!
> So rare a wondered father and a wise
> Makes this place paradise.

(4.1.122–4)

Though the folio version is clear enough in this regard, the eighteenth-century editor Nicholas Rowe substituted 'wife' for 'wise' in the second line on the commonsensical assumption that surely Ferdinand is at least as excited about the prospect of marrying Miranda as he is about acquiring Prospero as a father-in-law. Most modern editors have reverted to 'wise' prompting critics to speculate on Miranda's status in the marriage. Is she merely the object of exchange between the two men, Prospero and Ferdinand, necessary to cement their own relationship? Will she be relegated to the background of Ferdinand's life as Prospero's wife seems to have been by him? Textual cruces like this one are a reminder of how editorial choices can shift the meaning of a play in small but significant ways and how even print is a fluid, unfixed medium. As Andrew Murphy writes, 'Shakespeare editions always reflect the culture of the era in which they were produced. Alexander Pope fundamentally wanted a Shakespeare who was intelligible in the context of the aesthetic criteria of the early eighteenth century. We too have fashioned Shakespeare's text in our own image. Doubtless our successors will do just the same.' It is not easy to imagine what an edition of *The Tempest* might look like in a hundred or more years, especially with advances in online and digital editions. What is clear however is that generations have taken seriously the First Folio's editors' plea to 'reade him, therefore, and againe and againe'.

## *Reading* The Tempest – *identifying complexities*

Apart from textual cruces that are results of inscription, printing or editorial practices, the language of *The Tempest* is inherently complex. Some critics have maintained that ambiguity or the possibility of multiple meaning is the defining characteristic of the literary. In fact, it can be argued that literary language reveals the true nature of all language since ambiguity lies at the heart of all human linguistic communication for the simple reason that the relationship between the signifier and the signified, the expression and the meaning, is fundamentally arbitrary. Ambiguity can result from a writer's choice of words with many meanings or indeterminate meaning, from potentially misleading or confusing syntactical structures or from the manipulation of character, plot, setting and the other elements of narrative (all of which are, after all, still creations of language). It is through this evasiveness that meaning is made, or, to quote Shakespeare's *Hamlet*, readers 'by indirections finds directions out' (2.1.63). In fact, paradoxical as it might seem, the very slipperiness of poetic speech makes the truths it conveys all the more profound. As Paul de Man writes, 'poetry gains a maximum of convincing power at the very moment that it abdicates any claim to truth'.

*The Tempest* has conveyed several messages to readers across the ages. Although the word 'message' appears to imply that the play makes meaning in a fairly clear and straightforward manner, most readers would agree that few of these meanings are clear cut or singular. The play is best described as 'dialogic' or 'polyphonic' narrative. Such a narrative is one that allows multiple voices ('polyphonic') and points of view to emerge in the text without making any of them truly dominant. For Mikhail Bakhtin, the Russian formalist critic who first discussed the idea of polyphony and dialogism, these features are distinguishing characteristics of the literary. 'It is precisely the diversity of speech and not the unity of a normative shared language that is the ground of style', writes Bakhtin. This 'multi-voicededness' is also a matter of textual politics. Differing and even conflicting attitudes and world views get into dialogue (hence the term 'dialogic') or engage with each other and the text becomes a site of multiple contested meanings. The good reader is sensitive to the manifold layers of meaning and recognizes that the richness of a work like *The Tempest* and the fact that it has spoken to readers across centuries and cultures is due to its inherent complexity. In what follows, we will consider how ambiguity and dialogism inform certain aspects of the play and how it consistently defies simple or singular interpretation.

## *'Here in this island' – Language and landscape*

Though islands have moved the literary imagination before and since Shakespeare, *The Tempest* has Shakespeare's most famous island setting. The island suggests insularity and autonomy. It is a world unto itself and its very geography divides people into 'islanders' and 'outsiders'. The island also suggests solitude and a state of exile. In this, it serves as a figure for Prospero himself who is not only certainly lonely while on it, but was also solitary while in Milan, the magician-duke 'rapt in secret studies' (1.2.77). Like the mystical settings of romance literature, the island is a space of exile, the destination at the end of a turbulent journey and a place of refuge. After being betrayed at home and spending an undefined period at sea, Prospero tells Miranda, 'Here in this island we arrived' (1.2.171). Similarly, the island was Sycorax's place of banishment ('This blue-eyed hag was hither brought with child, / And here was left by th' sailors' (1.2.269–70)). It was also where she had a chance to live and give birth to her son.

Alonso, Ferdinand and their courtiers' response to the island is described in language that is conflicting and paradoxical. Ferdinand situates himself on it in these hauntingly beautiful lines: 'Sitting on a bank, / Weeping again the King my father's wreck, / This music crept by me upon the waters' (1.2.390–2). For Ferdinand, the island is the place of miraculous survival, but landing on it and finding himself alone, also forces him to acknowledge his father's death. The island becomes a space of mourning for him (as it is for Alonso), but then offers an indefinable beauty and even a strange peace in the midst of sorrow, for the music allays the fury of the waters 'and my passion / With its sweet air' (1.2.393–4). Eventually the island, again in the tradition of romance, becomes the space where the young romantic hero finds love.

The seductive and elusive language of the play, according to Alden and Virginia Mason Vaughan, 'creates the island's dreamlike effect, contributing to the audience's sense of suspension from time and place'. While this is correct, it is also true that the setting is described with a passion for detail almost unequalled in any of the other plays. The 'cloven pine' (1.2.77) with its 'knotty entrails' (1.2.295), the 'qualities o' th' isle' (1.2.338) that Caliban introduces to Prospero and his daughter, 'The fresh springs, brine pits, barren place and fertile' (1.2.339) are made incredibly vivid. Similarly, we are told of a 'filthy-mantled pool' (4.1.182) and 'fresh-brook mussels, withered roots, and husks / Wherein the acorn cradled' (1.2.464–5). Caliban promises to bring his second set of visitors, Stephano and Trinculo, to 'where crabs grow' to show them 'pignuts', 'a jay's nest', 'the nimble marmoset', 'clust'ring filberts' and 'young scamels from the rock' (2.2.164–9). While some of this wildlife defies classification and definition (generations of readers have wondered what on earth a 'scamel' is supposed to be), the language reads a little like entries from a naturalist's journal. This abundance and specificity of concrete nouns and adjectives makes the island landscape rich, lush and palpably real, even as it remains enchanted and mystical.

Readers have also felt the need to associate the island with a specific setting. It seems to be located somewhere in the Mediterranean (like the mystical islands of Virgil's *Aeneid*), going by the fact that Prospero's boat started out in Milan, and Alonso and party were attending a wedding in North Africa before the storm. But scholars eventually began to see *The Tempest* as Shakespeare's 'New World' play. In 1609, nine ships left England to settle Jamestown in Virginia, the first English colony in what is now the United States of America. One of them, the *Sea Venture*, encountered a storm near Bermuda and was given up for lost, though its passengers miraculously survived and reached Jamestown almost a year later. The so-called Bermuda Pamphlets, specifically *A Discovery of the Barmudas* by Sylvester Jourdain and a letter titled 'True Repertory of the Wrack' by William Strachey (both ca. 1610), survivors of the *Sea Venture*, are seen as sources for the play and Caliban has been read as a fictional representation of the New World native as perceived by Shakespeare. The play's references to the Caribbean god Setebos and the 'Behemothes' (possibly a reference to the Bermudas) have further influenced this reading. Consequently, the sense of wonder and excitement that characterizes the narratives of the 'voyages' of discovery makes its way into the play and is translated into the characters' experience of the magical, miraculous, frightening and beautiful. Ferdinand's exclamation on seeing Miranda, 'O, you wonder! / If you be maid or no' (1.2.427–8) and Alonso's discovery of his son alive and well are just two examples.

However, the excitement of the wondrous apart, struggles for land and resources also characterized English (or European) colonial ventures in the Americas. The power dynamics that informed this enterprise have consequently been read as the most relevant context for the play. The island is certainly the arena of a power struggle between Prospero and his former enemies, Prospero and Caliban, who each claims it as his own. It is subject to Prospero's strict governance and surveillance. Other colonial contexts have been identified as sources: Ireland, Africa, specifically North Africa and the Barbary coast. Arguments for and against each of these locations will be described in Chapter 3, but for now it will suffice to recognize that while it has been important for critics to identify the island as a specific and real historical space, the fact is that Shakespeare, like any good writer, superimposes multiple historical sites into his fictional island. In fact, as Barbara Fuchs writes, while 'placing New World colonialism at the centre of the play has made it fundamentally more interesting, and at least for twentieth-century readers, a more relevant text', recognizing the layering of a complex of sites and the possibility of multiple historical interpretations makes the play all the more rich and interesting.

The magic island is multifaceted in at least one other way. When the court party finds itself on the island, they respond to it in conflicting ways:

> ADRIAN Though this island seem to be desert –
> . . .
> Uninhabitable and almost inaccessible –
> SEBASTIAN Yet –
> ADRIAN Yet –
> ANTONIO He could not miss't.
> ADRIAN It must needs be of subtle, tender and delicate temperance.
> ANTONIO Temperance was a delicate wench.
> SEBASTIAN Ay, and a subtle, as he most learnedly delivered
> ADRIAN The air breathes upon us here most sweetly.
> SEBASTIAN As if it had lungs, and rotten ones.
> ANTONIO Or, as 'twere perfumed by a fen.
> GONZALO Here is everything advantageous to life.
> ANTONIO True, save means to live.
> SEBASTIAN Of that there's none, or little.
> GONZALO How lush and lusty the grass looks! How green!
> ANTONIO The ground indeed is tawny.
>
> (2.1.37–56)

In effect, the courtiers are not seeing the same island; the landscape each one describes deliberately contradicts the other's. The lines quoted above are a series of obvious oppositions. The grass of the island, for instance, is green to some of the voyagers and 'tawny' to others. The idealistic Gonzalo sees a land full of rich possibility while the more cynical courtiers can see only sterility and despair. The setting thus becomes a projection of the characters' personality or, more interestingly, the language used by individual characters to describe the world around them structures their experience of the world. This reading has been historically situated by

John Gillies who argues that the Renaissance English discourse of Virginia was characterized by both 'plenty and
famine'. Voyagers described the colony as dank and disease
infested even as they paradoxically saw it as a temperate
space of sustenance and fertility. There was both optimism
and pessimism regarding the potential of the newfound land,
just as Shakespeare's island represents danger, ruthless power
struggle and loss, even as it represents hope and deliverance.
Gonzalo's optimism stands in paradoxical relationship with
the other courtiers' cynicism and complicates our vision of the
island even as it draws attention to the fact that the language
of paradox, as Cleanth Brooks argues, is 'appropriate and
inevitable to poetry'. Literature juxtaposes words and utterances in new and unpredictable ways and consequently the
truths it expresses and the meanings it makes are also unexpected and sometimes even disruptive. In a famous speech,
Gonzalo reflects on the ideal commonwealth he would create
if he had 'plantation of this isle':

> I' th' commonwealth I would by contraries
> Execute all things, for no kind of traffic
> Would I admit; no name of magistrate;
> Letters should not be known; riches, poverty
> And use of service, none; contract, succession,
> Bourn, bound of land, tilth, vineyard – none;
> No use of metal, corn, or wine or oil;
> No occupation, all men idle, all;
> And women, too, but innocent and pure;
> No sovereignity –
> ----------------------------
> All things in common nature should produce
> Without sweat or endeavour; treason, felony,
> Sword, pike, knife, gun, or need of any engine
> Would I not have; but nature should bring forth
> Of its own kind all foison, all abundance,
> To feed my innocent people.

(2.1.148–57, 160–5)

The lines echo the French writer Michel de Montaigne's essay 'Of the Cannibals' in which he contrasts European corruption and degeneracy to the innocence and culture of Brazilian Indians (and American natives generally speaking). The 'New World' (evoked here by Gonzalo's use of the word 'plantation') was often viewed as an Edenic space where mankind could start afresh. Gonzalo's vision recognizes that in order to build the ideal commonwealth he'd have to do things by 'contraries' or in opposition to received practice. The language of the speech is characterized by negation ('no', 'none'); the commonwealth is clearly defined by the absence of the institutions and systems – riches, poverty, property, labour, service, inheritance, kingship – that burden so-called civilized society. Gonzalo's rhetoric not only echoes many other Renaissance discourses of utopia (interestingly utopias – ideal societies or communities as envisioned by thinkers – were often located on islands, as in Thomas More's 1516 book *Utopia*) but also reflects a universal and timeless need to envision and strive towards the perfect society. As Oscar Wilde wrote centuries later, 'A map of the world that does not include utopia is not worth even glancing at, for it leaves out the one country at which Humanity is always landing. And Humanity when it lands there, it looks out, and seeing a better country, sets sail.'

However, it is possible to debate the meaning of Gonzalo's lines. He might be being too naive and far too optimistic. The abstractions that fill his speech certainly emphasize his idealism and perhaps his lack of worldliness. His listeners in the play certainly think so. Sebastian and Antonio point out contradictions in his vision ('The latter end of his commonwealth forgets the beginning' (2.1.159)) and mock the old courtier. And even the sympathetic reader would concede that Gonzalo is prone to being somewhat garrulous and occasionally simplistic in his views. His vision of a commonwealth ruled by virtue and innocence seems especially misguided given that the villainous Antonio and Sebastian will soon attempt to execute their treacherous plans. Gonzalo privileges 'nature' and its 'abundance' and sees it as an engine of change and assumes the purity and innocence of men and women, while the play seems to depict that humans are 'naturally' evil and it is Prospero's 'art' (in contrast to 'nature') that can bring about reform, penitence and salvation. However, Gonzalo is the most generous hearted and endearing of characters in the play and those who jeer at him are among the most unambiguously evil. Surely, his vision, however romantic and far-fetched, even impossible, needs to be admired for the conviction and sincerity with which it is articulated by the loyal old courtier? Perhaps, there *is* something to it.

The play refuses to resolve this debate. It is left to the reader to piece together the author's depiction of character and situation as well as the language of the speech in order to understand the vision of the play. For instance, is the long, detailed nature of the speech an endorsement of the views expressed? Or does the very same lengthiness, the spelling out of details, the excess of abstract nouns, the haphazard juxtaposition of the economic, moral and social, point toward the ridiculousness of the unreal scope and expanse of Gonzalo's vision? If Gonzalo's version stands in paradoxical relationship with Sebastian's and Antonio's cynicism, what exactly does this tell us about the island and about literary language itself?

The island setting is full of possibilities and Shakespeare does not fail to explore all of them to some degree. There is only one character native to the island (Caliban). Everyone else has come to it. But even the outsiders cannot leave, or have nowhere else to go. Themes of belonging, loss and displacement – very relevant to modern readers – are complicated right away and further explored through the representation of the two central characters, Prospero and Caliban.

## *Representing the hero – Prospero*

Prospero has long been identified as the play's central consciousness. Fiction sets up a central narrative voice, a point of view from which a story is told, but what about drama? What aspect of a play's language and structure makes it possible to identify the 'main character' as opposed to 'secondary characters'? What is it about the way that *The Tempest* is written that has made many readers identify with Prospero and see it as primarily his story? Why do we take more of an interest in his fortunes and wish him well? The playwright might have achieved these effects by devoting more space to Prospero than to any other character. He appears in six out of the nine scenes in the play and dominates them. This alone might serve to make him the protagonist of the play and its dominant consciousness. While Shakespeare does not use in this play the dramatic device of the soliloquy, which he often turns to in order to create a sense of intimacy between reader and character, Prospero is assigned lengthier speeches written in a more elevated poetic style (the 'Our revels are now ended' speech in 4.1 is a prominent example). Besides, he is introduced to us after the noise and chaos of the storm scene, and though it is Miranda who speaks first, it is Prospero who is clearly established as the more authoritative voice and is consequently the first character who imposes himself on the readers' consciousness in a coherent way. His opening scene is worth considering in some detail.

Prospero responds to Miranda's distress calmly but not callously. His opening lines 'Be collected, / No more amazement. Tell your piteous heart / There's no harm done' (1.2.14–15) are kept deliberately short and simple. The language conveys a gentleness and firmness that is appealing and Prospero seems the perfect father. And when he adds that 'I have done nothing but in care of thee, / Of thee, my dear one, thee my daughter'(1.2.16–17), the language of endearment, along with the insistent repetition ('of thee, of thee . . . thee', 'my . . . my' and 'I am . . . I am') ensures that we pay attention to him and also, quite simply, like him. This effect is further achieved by the culminating lines: 'I am more better / Than Prospero, master of a full poor cell, / And thy no greater father' (1.2. 18–21). The lines pique the reader's curiosity. What cell? What is Prospero going to reveal? Renaissance readers expected their heroes to be high born, and though there is no evidence yet that Prospero is a nobleman, his elevated style of speech and the hints he throws out so early in the scene hold out the promise that he well might be. And we all tend to sympathize with a hero who is down and out in the world, especially when he doesn't deserve to be.

Having chosen Prospero's first few lines carefully, Shakespeare has him launch into a long narrative that explains how he came to be on the island. The plot line of the usurping brother recurs in many of Shakespeare's plays (*As You Like It*, *Hamlet*) and sympathy is always directed towards the sibling done out of his rights. Antonio is described as 'false', with an 'evil nature', and as devious and manipulating, while Prospero can only be blamed for being too trusting, for having a 'confidence sans bound' in his brother (1.2.97). Above all, Prospero is associated with the study of magic. He therefore cuts a striking figure, this mysterious scholar-ruler who was 'rapt in secret studies' and who devoted his life to the quest of a learning that is esoteric, and also worthy and important.

Writing this account of Prospero's pre-island past must have been more difficult to execute than it first appears. Not only does Shakespeare have to set up his hero, but he also has to encapsulate events that took place over many years in a few brief lines and render them immediate and interesting. A lesser writer might have lost his audience. But after convincing us of Antonio's treachery, Shakespeare describes Prospero's escape from Milan. With the loyal Gonzalo and a weeping, motherless infant, he sets out of gates of Milan 'i' th' dead of darkness', the boat they embarked was a 'rotten carcass of a butt' and pushes out to 'cry to' th' sea' and 'sigh/ To th' winds' (1.2.130, 146, 149–50). By manipulating visual and auditory imagery, the scene is invested with a vividness and drama that is really quite unsurpassable and that fills the reader with pity and fear for the wronged man and his hapless child.

Their hazardous voyage to seemingly nowhere is a skilful rewriting of the romance motif of the heroic journey. But the voyage of the romance hero, while always perilous, is purposeful and leads to his personal and spiritual regeneration. In the Strachey document describing the journey to Virginia, the party has to endure a 'dreadful storm and hideous' but the Bermudas 'hideous and hated' as they are also 'the place of our safety and means of our deliverance', therefore, illustrating God's mercy. Prospero's journey to the island is also described in these dual terms. When Miranda asks him if the banishment was only a result of foul play or if, in some mysterious way, the fact that they had to leave was a blessing, Prospero replies, 'Both, both, my girl' (1.2.61). Like the romance hero's adventures, the outcome and meaning of Prospero's journey are determined by God. Suffering is framed in paradoxical terms as what is termed *felix culpa* or suffering that led to redemption and realizing God, a framework that Shakespeare often turns to in the tragedies. Prospero's travails have already led him to appreciate Gonzalo's loyalty and will possibly lead to his own moral and spiritual growth. This depiction of Prospero renders him human and sympathetic, and also more profound and interesting. He becomes a symbol of suffering humanity itself. Prospero goes on to tell Miranda that he has conjured the storm deliberately, and eventually, he will go on to direct the course of the plot and scripts the fates of other characters. He will, in a sense, be the author's representative in the play. The reader is thus left with an impression of a wise, benign protagonist, who is solitary, but brave and intelligent, who is using all the powers at his disposal to dispense justice and right the wrongs inflicted on himself and on his child. What better hero?

This opening dialogue is however structured in such a way as to allow for quite a different reading. The fact that Prospero takes control of the narrative can be seen as a sign of his dominance and need for control. He orders Miranda to 'Obey and be attentive' and proceeds to ask her, 'Canst thou remember / A time before we came unto the cell?' (1.2.38–9). He then proceeds to answer the question himself, 'I do not think thou canst' (1.2.40). While it would be an exaggeration to say that he dismisses Miranda's response outright, <u>Prospero does take</u> <u>control over memory and the act of recounting the past</u>, and we ultimately have only his account of what happened in Milan. However, even as he can be seen as the benevolent philosopher-duke, he can also be perceived as negligent of his duties as ruler. He after all 'grew stranger' (1.2.76) to the state and while here is perhaps something appealing about one for whom 'my library / Was dukedom large enough' (1.2.109–10), the verb in his confession to 'neglecting worldly ends' (1.2.89) signals that Prospero's failure as ruler has been quite obviously his own fault, a fact he is reluctant to admit to outright. Antonio comes across as the more dynamic, and to him is ascribed the ability to remake and manipulate those around him. In a sense he too is a magician, even an artist, as implied by the line, he 'new created / The creatures that were mine . . . or changed 'em' (1.2.81–2). Besides, Prospero very oddly interrupts his own narrative repeatedly: 'Dost thou attend me?' he asks Miranda (1.2.78), and after she assures him that indeed she has been attending to him, he continues his narrative but halts again to reprimand her: 'Thou attend'st not!' (1.2.87). This pattern is repeated at least once more when he asks, 'Dost thou hear?' and she responds (with a touch of barely discernable irony?) that his tale 'would cure deafness' (1.2.106). This sequence of exchanges when coupled with Prospero's irregular, jerky lines gives the impression that the benign, all-powerful magician is not only agitated, but is also perhaps somewhat insecure of his control over narrative and perhaps over his daughter as well.

Prospero's conversations with other characters are equally subject to multiple, even contradictory readings. In his exchange with Ariel, he can be read as the generous master who saved Ariel from a terrible fate (and Prospero's description of the 'delicate' spirit's predicament vividly conveys the horror of being trapped in a cloven pine for years). Ariel's simple answer 'I thank thee, master' (1.2.293) is genuine in its expression of gratitude and confirms Prospero's story. Prospero's righteous indignation at what he perceives as the ingratitude of a servant who will not stay out his contract seems fully justified. At the same time, here too, Prospero takes charge of narrative and memory: 'Remember I have done thee worthy service', he says (1.2.247), and once again, 'Dost thou forget . . . Hast thou forgot . . .?' (1.2.250, 257). He will, he insists, remind Ariel once every month of what he's done for him. These lines make Prospero seem annoying at the very least, and domineering and unjust at worst. The same uncontrolled fury is discernable when he lashes out at Ariel (who is first addressed as 'my brave spirit' (1.2.206) and in other equally loving terms): 'Thou liest, malignant thing' (1.2.257).

Prospero's first interaction with Caliban can serve to reinforce Prospero's goodness and heroism. Prospero's description of Caliban sets us up to dislike the latter even before his entrance. He is a 'freckled whelp, hag-born' (1.2.283) and a 'slave', in contrast to Prospero's natural dignity as high-born aristocrat and wise magician. The fact that Caliban's first words are a series of vicious though colourful curses does not help his case either and there is nothing to salvage his reputation when we hear that he was used 'with humane care' (1.2.347) before he sought to violate Miranda's honour. This is a charge that Caliban does not deny and even crudely gloats over saying if he hadn't been prevented he 'had peopled else / This isle with Calibans' (1.2.351–2), further confirming that Prospero is speaking the truth. Our good wishes are most likely to be with Prospero as Caliban lumbers offstage.

However, once again, Shakespeare's scripting of the scene is complicated and provokes readers to question and revise their own responses to the text. He inserts a detail that forces us to take another look at Prospero's place on the island. In recounting past history to Miranda, Prospero dwells at length on the events in Milan but glosses over his arrival on the island with a neutral: 'Here in this island we arrived' (1.2.171). Caliban, however, complicates and contests this account of history. If Prospero is anxious to remind Miranda and Ariel of the past, here it is Caliban who does the recalling: 'This island's mine by Sycorax, my mother, / Which thou

tak'st from me' (1.2.32–33). The language of the speech that
follows is passionate, yet powerful and elegant, in contrast
to Prospero's rather lengthy and somewhat disjointed narrative of the past. Caliban's claim is voiced in a simple and
direct manner. Prospero's earlier behaviour towards Caliban
(when he petted and 'made much' of him) is mentioned to
highlight the injustice of his later behaviour when he confines
Caliban to a rock (following so soon after the narrative of
the imprisoning of Ariel in the cloven pine, this detail sets
up a parallel between Prospero and Sycorax). Caliban ends
his speech as simply as he began it: he is restricted to a hard
rock 'whiles you do keep from me / The rest o' th' island'
(1.2.344–5). The sheer wrongness of this is undeniable and
for all his insistence on the legitimacy of power it seems like
Prospero, the usurped ruler, does not hesitate to appropriate another's rights, however much he might be reluctant to
describe his settlement of the island in these terms. At this
point in the play, at least momentarily, it is Caliban who has
taken possession of the narrative and insists on the validity of
his version of history. Prospero responds by denying Caliban's
charge (rather weakly and maybe somewhat hysterically) and
by throwing a counter-accusation of attempted rape. For
those critics who read *The Tempest* as the Shakespeare play
that enacts or is at least informed by the discourses of colonialism (this critical trend will be elaborated on in Chapter
3), Prospero is the prototype of the colonizer who not only
takes possession of land, but also has the power to insist on
his construction of events as the truth, while Caliban is the
native who dares to talk back. In any case, Caliban never
fails to upset Prospero in some deep and profound way. When
Caliban appears, Prospero is filled with anger, indulges in
self-pity or moves between the two as conveyed in the lines
'A devil, a born devil, on whose nature / Nurture can never
stick; on whom my pains / Humanely taken – all, all, lost,
quite lost!' (4.1.188–90). Even as he is the most obvious symbol and object of Prospero's power, Caliban is also the force
that most frequently challenges it.

*The Tempest* continues to repeat this ambivalent structure through the narrative. The indeterminate representation of Prospero's magic has also led to much critical debate. How do we read the fact that Prospero can conjure up storms, but apparently could not use his powers of enchantment to save himself while in Milan, or, for that matter, to fetch his own wood and make his own fires? Did the move to the island quicken the magic and move it beyond mere book learning? Is putting Caliban to work simply a means of humiliating him, rather than any real dependence on his labour? Is Prospero's magic an admirable and in some sense more 'modern' kind of power because, unlike his ducal power, it is self-created and comes from individual labour rather than inheritance? Or does that same feature make it a mark of his Faustian arrogance?

Most importantly, what exactly is this magic? Some scholars have made specific associations between Prospero's 'liberal arts' and the great traditions of Renaissance magic, that foreshadowed science and envisioned moral and religious reform. Prospero has been associated with the Renaissance Hermetic philosopher Henry Corneius Agrippa and with John Dee, the mathematician-magician who was Elizabeth I's astrologer but who fell out of favour under King James. Most often, however, Prospero's art has more generally been viewed simply as 'white magic'. Frank Kermode's opinion represents the popular critical view that Prospero's magic was 'the disciplined exercise of virtuous knowledge' that was used to reform and that helped him acquire the virtues of discipline and self-restraint. However, Prospero's own account of the events in Milan indicates that magic however 'good' and reformative it might have been, was a self-indulgence, and eventually proved dangerous to himself and his rule. Prospero seems to have recognized the potential of magic as a political instrument on the island and uses it to establish and maintain his power. Magic split the cloven pine that freed Ariel, and Caliban is frightened of and persecuted by Prospero's spirits. Caliban also recognizes that Prospero's power comes through knowledge when he intersperses his vision of the violence he wishes enacted upon Prospero's person with the repeated injunction to 'Burn but his books' (3.2.95).

The 'goodness' of Prospero's magic is also thrown into question. He first describes his pursuit of magic as 'secret studies'. The qualifier 'secret' might denote the esoteric nature of his scholarship, but it might also imply that it is a pursuit that needs to be practiced covertly. Renaissance readers and viewers might not have been as certain of the nobility and morally elevated nature of Prospero's magic as subsequent audiences have been. In the final act when Prospero decides to give up his magic, he outlines its potency:

> Ye elves of hills, brooks, standing lakes and groves,
> And ye that on the sands with printless foot
> Do chase the ebbing Neptune, and do fly him
> When he comes back; you demi-puppets that
> By moonshine do the green sour ringlets make,
> Whereof the ewe not bites; and you whose pastime
> Is to make the midnight-mushrooms, that rejoice
> To hear the solemn curfew, by whose aid –
> Weak masters though ye be – I have bedimmed
> The noontide sun, called forth the mutinous winds,
> And 'twixt the green sea and the azured vault
> Set roaring war; to the dread rattling thunder
> Have I given fire and rifted Jove's stout oak
> With his own bolt: the strong-based promontory
> Have I made shake, and by the spurs plucked up
> The pine and cedar; graves at my command
> Have waked their speakers, ope'd and let 'em forth
> By my so potent art.
>
> (5.1.33–50)

The imagery in this masterfully executed speech is both fantastic (elves dancing on seashores with 'printless foot', the little folk who make 'green sour ringlets' by moonlight) and grand ('the green sea and the azured vault' at war, the 'noontide sun' in eclipse). This, coupled with the run-on lines and quaint compound words ('midnight-mushrooms', 'demi-puppets'), seduces the reader into believing in the powerful and positive force that is Prospero's magic. We *want* to believe in its innate benevolence. But the images become progressively darker and culminate in the chilling 'graves at my command / Have wak'd their sleepers, ope'd and let 'em forth'. The elves and 'demi-puppets' too are not simply curious little creatures that assist Prospero but are also 'masters' over their own spheres and perhaps over him. Magic is admittedly never part of the familiar or everyday, but turning to Shklovsky's idea of 'defamiliarization' outlined in the introductory chapter, these lines serve to 'defamiliarize' Prospero's magic for even those of us who have become habituated to it and have started to see it as one of the many fantastical elements in the play. All of a sudden, it is now darker and more mysterious. Renaissance audiences most likely did not relegate magic to the pages of children's books and to folk superstition, but viewed it as a real force that wielded a power that could potentially touch people's lives. They might have disapproved of Prospero's dalliance with ungodly forces as much as they would have been troubled by his reference to waking the dead, a power specifically associated with black magic. Prospero's speech is a paraphrase of the witch Medea's speech in the Roman writer Ovid's work *Metamorphosis* (in Greek myth Medea was an enchantress and prophetess who helped the hero Jason and eventually married him. He left her for another woman. In Book VII of *Metamorphosis*, Ovid depicts her taking revenge on Jason). Medea's speech was, in the words of Jonathan Bate, 'viewed in the Renaissance as witch-craft's set piece'. In an age in which the witch manifested the worst kind of demonic power (doubly evil because it was feminized), Prospero's echo of Medea marks his 'potent art' as drawing upon dark energies that no Christian could approve of. So, even as Prospero is anxious to separate himself from Sycorax's 'mischiefs manifold and sorceries terrible' (1.2.264), his magic might not be all that different from hers.

His powers too might have been derived from forces that the original audience would have viewed with some suspicion, if not fear.

After laying out the awe-inspiring capacities of his 'potent art', Prospero rather unexpectedly announces that he will give it up:

> But this rough magic
> I here abjure; and when I have required
> Some heavenly music (which even now I do)
> To work mine end upon their senses that
> This airy charm is for, I'll break my staff,
> Bury it certain fathoms in the earth,
> And deeper than did ever plummet sound
> I'll drown my book.
>
> (5.1.50–7)

Apart from its significance to the plot of *The Tempest*, this speech is often read as Shakespeare bidding farewell to the stage. In Prospero's 'revels' speech in Act 4, Shakespeare has pondered the illusory and transient nature of the art he had practiced for so long and so brilliantly. In this speech, he speaks once again through Prospero, who is among his last and most complex poetic creations. Prospero, like Shakespeare, is an aging man who has decided to return home, and his 'rough magic' is Shakespeare's art. In contrast to the first half of the speech, the declaration of the relinquishment of magic (or theatre) does not rely on magnificent rhetoric for effect. Instead, the announcement to give up what has been a lifelong passion and source of power and identity is made with a quietness that makes the renunciation even more dignified and admirable than the pursuit. The word 'but' prepares the reader for a shift in mood from the drama and arrogance discernable in the earlier lines. The single long sentence is broken up into elegant shorter segments: 'But this rough magic / I'll here abjure', 'I'll break my staff' and 'I'll drown my book'. Rather than a long, melodramatic statement that resorts to ponderous abstractions

such as sacrifice and renunciation, Shakespeare describes
Prospero's decision through the two vivid and very concrete
images of breaking his staff and drowning his book (both of
which have now become widely used metaphors for renunciation of power). The deliberate vagueness of 'certain fathoms'
nicely offsets the more dramatic simile 'deeper than did ever
plummet sound'. The words 'break', 'bury' and 'drown' are
skilful choices of verb. They signify the finality of the act, and
because 'bury' and 'drown' are associated with the death of
living things we also get the sense that Prospero's art is an
intimate companion (his only one other than his daughter)
and giving it up is akin to acknowledging and coming to terms
with the death of a loved one whom, ironically he needs to
kill himself. The three verbs indicate the violence as well as
the poignancy of his action. The adjective 'rough' in 'rough
magic' is more puzzling. The editors of the third Arden edition of the play explain it as Prospero giving up 'his power to
wreak physical harm'. They add that '*Rough* can be taken in a
more benign sense, meaning "rudely sufficient", . . . Prospero
could be self-deprecating here, referring to the imperfect
nature of his craft'. They also offer a third interpretation, 'the
preceding allusions to Medea's incantation suggests to us that
the adjective *rough* here indicates the underlying danger of
the magus' power.' The word 'rough' could then be Prospero's
own admission to the dubious nature of his art. It also invites
one to ponder what exactly he is giving up. Has he decided to
give up a crude form of power for a more sophisticated form
of control? As he goes back to being a duke, is he reclaiming a
political power that is more subtle, maybe even more devious,
in its practice? But will the self-confessed scholar ever be a
successful politician? The play lets the reader ponder this and
other questions.

As *The Tempest* draws to its end, Gonzalo claims that while
the young people have found love in the course of this sea
voyage, everyone else found themselves. Has Prospero found
himself? It can be argued that the play follows a gradually
changing protagonist. We have already seen a Prospero who

understands the nature and practice of political power better than he did in his Milan days. In the tradition of *felix culpa*, Prospero should emerge wiser and stronger in a more profound spiritual sense as well. Even those readers who would say that the language of the play depicts Prospero as wise and heroic, would concede that if he has a fault at the beginning of the play it is an unfortunate tendency toward anger and the more problematic inability to forgive his enemies. It is Ariel who later points out to him the way of mercy. He tells Prospero that Alonso and company wander the island 'Brimful of sorrow and dismay' (5.1.14). If Prospero could catch a glimpse of them, he too would feel pity for them. 'Dost thou think so, spirit?' Prospero asks (5.1.18). The interrogative at this point is telling; Prospero is either puzzled by the idea of compassion, or half-surprised that it is even possible that he can be expected to experience it. Ariel says his affections would certainly be moved 'were I human' (5.1.20). At that, Prospero, soon after his decision to abjure magic, takes his second resolution:

> And mine shall.
> Hast thou, which art but air, a touch, a feeling
> Of their afflictions, and shall not myself
> (One of their kind, that relish all as sharply,
> Passion as they) be kindlier moved than thou art?
> Though with their high wrongs I am struck to th' quick,
> Yet with their nobler reason 'gainst my fury
> Do I take part. The rarer action is
> In virtue than in vengeance. They being penitent,
> The sole drift of my purpose doth extend
> Not a frown further.
>
> (5.1.20–30)

The speech is not as vivid or as well executed as the one relinquishing magic. The lines are somewhat metrically irregular and the involved syntax indicates that Prospero has some difficulty accepting and giving voice to the virtues of clemency. But the sentence that stands out is 'The rarer action is / In virtue than in vengeance.' Prospero has moved towards a recognition of the futility of revenge. Forgiveness is the 'rarer action', less observed and more difficult. Eventually, Prospero does come face to face with his associates from Naples and Milan. He does not forget to express his gratitude to Gonzalo for past favours and delights in leading the mourning Alonso to his son. He graciously tells the king that they should not 'burden our remembrances with / A heaviness that is gone' (5.1.199–200) – wise words from one who obsessively dwelt on the past and its injustices. Prospero even forgives his brother, perhaps.

The play is ambiguous in its treatment of this last point. Prospero makes it clear to Antonio and Sebastian that he does know of their treacherous plot to assassinate the king and adds: 'At this time / I will tell no tales' (5.1.128–9). It is up to the reader to decide, in the context of the rest of the play, if this should be read as a promise or a threat. It is equally difficult to pin down the tone of his public speech to Antonio:

> For you, most wicked sir, whom to call brother
> Would even infect my mouth, I do forgive
> Thy rankest fault – all of them; and require
> My dukedom of thee, which perforce I know
> Thou must restore.
>
> (5.1.130–4)

Quite rightfully, Prospero reclaims his dukedom. That he does so with little ceremony or subtlety (he makes it quite clear that Antonio has no choice in the matter) is also perhaps understandable. The speech is as much one of denunciation as it is of forgiveness, however. Prospero reserves and publicly uses some of his harshest language for his brother and announces his pardon even as he makes it clear that the faults were many and of the 'rankest' order (in fact, the language of putrefaction and disease dominates this speech). Once again, we are left wondering whether this is a speech of forgiveness at all, and if it is, how wholehearted and complete is Prospero's mercy.

Does the memory of past wrongs overcome him even as he attempts to forgive? Is he filled with a sense of his own righteousness and benevolence? Isn't this too a form of ego? And most importantly perhaps, if one answers these questions in the affirmative, isn't Prospero being simply human? Perhaps, the point is to demonstrate that even this magician-duke is no god.

If Prospero's narrative dominated the first act of the play, this final act ends with his promising to tell the newcomers to the island 'the story of my life, / And particular accidents gone by / Since I came to this isle –' (5.1.305–7). Once again, Prospero will take over narrative. But this desire to dominate discourse seems to be overshadowed by the desire for contemplation and rest.

The epilogue to *The Tempest*, which is spoken by Prospero (or the actor who plays Prospero), is not strictly necessary to the play's action and might have been added by Shakespeare for special productions (the doggerel-like metre and simple vocabulary even make Shakespeare's authorship of these lines questionable). It includes the request for applause typical of many Renaissance epilogues, and once again quite explicitly connects Shakespeare's dramatic art to Prospero's magical arts. Prospero simply announces, with no obvious relief or regret, that his 'charms are all o'erthrown' (Epilogue 1). He also returns to the rhetoric of bondage and liberty that has dominated the play. Like Caliban, Ariel and other servants, Prospero/Shakespeare too has been 'confined' by the audience and pleads for his release. By describing his aim as just 'to please' (Epilogue 13), both the author and/or Prospero talk of their respective arts with a humility that is almost self-deprecatory. Here, Prospero's magic is no longer about waking the dead or even reforming fellow men, it simply becomes about gratifying viewers, just as the ultimate aim of Shakespeare's theatre is to keep the audience entertained. The last few lines of the epilogue strive for a balance between a deep sense of sorrow, if not despair ('Now I want / Spirits to enforce, art to enchant' (Epilogue 13–14)) and the tranquillity that comes from faith. If one wants to read the Epilogue as the character Prospero's speech (and not just the author speaking through Prospero), the domineering, irascible personality of the five acts of the play has been effectively written out and what we have is a gentle, wise older man who has decided that 'Every third thought shall be my grave' (5.1.312).

## Language and rebellion – Caliban

Caliban is among the extraordinary of Shakespeare's creations, a superb product of the 'dialogic imagination'. He is the villain to Prospero's hero, yet has some claims to heroism himself; his language is crude and marked by hostility and fear, yet it is also among the most lyrical in the play and indicates an exquisitely developed sensibility; he is treacherous and violent, and yet can be viewed as standing for the passion and energy behind all calls for positive social change. Shakespeare has invested his entire prowess with language into realizing Caliban, and it requires careful and sensitive reading to understand this character in all his wonderful complexity.

Caliban's name is an anagram for 'cannibal' (though we see him eating nothing more bloody than berries, fruits and fish). He is described in the Folio's 'Names of Actors' as a 'savage and deformed slave'. The word 'slave' is used variously in Shakespeare – it not only stands for a person in a state of subjugation, but also signifies anyone who is villainous and base (as in the case of Iago in *Othello*). The 'savage man' who lived outside of civilization is a figure in literature dating back to the Middle Ages, and Caliban has clearly been influenced by this tradition. He emerges from the monstrous and malformed creatures that appear in mythology of all traditions, as well as from Renaissance travellers' tales of the oddly shaped humans who supposedly inhabited other parts of the world. More recently, Caliban has been read as the author's representation of the native of the 'New World' (after all his name does associate him with the Caribbean and he makes reference to

Setebos, a South American god), but as some critics have been anxious to point out, there are almost no details in the play (no reference to arrows, or body paint or animal hide clothing, for instance) to make any such connection. Alden Vaughan points out that while the play does not identify Caliban as an Indian per se, the play does 'imply an affinity between Shakespeare's "savage and deformed" slave and a prevalent, pejorative view of American natives'. Vaughan explains that several dozen natives of the Americas, as well as Eskimos, spent varying periods of time in London in Shakespeare's lifetime and they might have inspired the author in some way.

It may be quite unnecessary to precisely identify Caliban's racial or ethnic identity, what matters is that he represents moral and cultural difference against which Prospero is constructed. It is Caliban's presence that has provoked many critics to see *The Tempest* as the Shakespeare play that best explores issues of colonial oppression. Again, the play may or may not be 'about' the political and historical project that we today describe as 'colonialism' or 'imperialism', but it does engage with attitudes to otherness and cultural and racial difference that formed the ideological basic of the colonial enterprise.

The play employs a colourful range of vocabulary to describe Caliban. He is 'freckled whelp' (1.2.283), a 'villain' (1.2.310), a 'tortoise' (1.2.317), 'a poisonous slave, got by the devil himself' (1.2.320), 'A thing most brutish' (1.2.358), of a 'vile race' (1.2.359), 'hag-seed' (1.2.366), 'mooncalf' (2.2.105), ' most scurvy monster' (2.2.152), 'misshapen knave' (5.1.268) and a 'thing of darkness' (5.1.275). These terms associate him with the bestial, suggest a grotesque hybridity and signal his immoral state and his unnatural birth. In the tradition of romance where evil within is represented by ugliness without, he is described 'as disproportioned in his manners / As in his shape' (5.1.291–2). While Ariel is the delicate airy spirit, Caliban is all gross materiality, and if Prospero stands for intellect, art, or even just humanity in all its complexity, Caliban is matter in all its crudeness and simplicity (he is described as both 'earth' and 'filth' (1.2.315, 347)). He is also the monstrous contrast to the handsome and good Ferdinand who stands out for his chastity, hard work and self-control. In the manner of the traditional villain, Caliban's role seems to be to set off the goodness of the righteous characters and to hinder them in the pursuit of their desires and happiness.

But almost immediately, Shakespeare problematizes this representation of his villain. There is no way to tell if this is a sign of the author's political sensitivity or his unwillingness to dismiss other races as inhuman. What we can say with greater certainty is that Caliban is an indication of a tremendous literary talent at work. Shakespeare knew that an evil villain is not necessarily an interesting character to write or read, so he presents us a profound and complex personality who fills us with repulsion and dismay even as he moves us; who makes a mockery of stereotypes as much as he reinforces them.

As discussed on page 43, Caliban's simple and powerfully worded claim to the island offsets the curses we hear him mouth as he makes his entrance in Act 1. His claim is through the maternal line (unlike the others in the play who validate only the paternal) and he contrasts Prospero's earlier kindness to him to his later injustices and cruelties. Shakespeare invests Caliban with great linguistic prowess. In a single speech, he combines both anger and pain with an elegance and passion reminiscent of that other Shakespearean 'villain', Shylock. When Caliban says, 'This island is mine by Sycorax, my mother', we are not only reminded of his right to the land, but the careful placement of 'mother' at the end of the line forcefully also reminds us that this monstrous creature is someone's child, and that Sycorax is not only a malignant witch but also a mother. Similarly, 'And I then I loved thee' (1.2.337) is placed at the end of a line to show the spontaneity and purity of Caliban's response to Prospero. We cannot help but think of an orphaned child alone on the island, eager to please and anxious to be loved by the newcomers. He was treated as human at first by Prospero, perhaps even *made* human and then rejected as subhuman. Caliban's speech culminates in the spat-out exclamation 'Cursed be I that did so!' (1.2.340). As we saw, Prospero's response to these lines can easily be read as weak and self-defensive. However, his accusation of Caliban's attempted rape of Miranda complicates any sympathy we might have started to feel for Caliban, especially because Caliban's admission to the crime is crude and aggressive: 'O ho, O ho! Would't had been done; / Thou didst prevent me, I had peopled else / This isle with Calibans' (1.2.350–3). At this point, we too are inclined to agree with Miranda's statement that he was 'Deservedly confined into this rock' (1.2.362).

However, that is not the singular impression we are left with. Caliban's protests against injustice still ring in our ears and we are left confused and unsure of how to feel about this strange being. Do we sympathize with him or not? Is the play typical of colonial discourse in its vilification of the native, or does it actually highlight his virtues? Caliban might be 'only' a slave, but as Prospero himself admits, he is indispensible to them and without him there would be no one to fetch wood, make fire or serve 'in offices / That profit us' (1.2.313–14). Is Caliban's suffering from the cramps and pinches he constantly complains of comic and ludicrous, or pitiful? Though he is accused again and again of being stubborn and immune to reform ('A devil, a born devil, on whose nature / Nurture can never stick' (4.1.188–9)), we get the sense of a flexible, ever-altering, vibrant personality.

'Where the devil should he learn our language?' (2.2.65–6) Stephano wonders on encountering Caliban. The monster slave uses language not just proficiently but also to poetic effect. The poet John Dryden wrote that 'Caliban's language is as hobgoblin as his person'. Although Dryden has little that is complimentary to say about Caliban's personality (he remarks that Caliban 'has all the discontents and malice of a witch or a devil . . . gluttony, sloth and lust are manifest') and he probably does not intend 'hobgoblin' as an accolade either, it is true that Caliban's language is unique and idiosyncratic. His speeches are never as lengthy as Prospero's, but they cannot be mistaken

for anyone else's in the play. Even his curses are characterized by vivid images and as infused with fantasy as anything
uttered by Ariel. The sheer beauty of his language also lingers.
He talks of the sun and the moon as the 'bigger light and . . .
the less / That burn by day and night' (1.2.336–7), and his language reaches heights of lyricism when he refers to the natural
landscape of the island, what he calls the 'qualities o' th' isle'
(1.2.338). His invocation of 'fresh springs, brine pits, barren
place and fertile' (1.2.339) and his later promise 'to bring thee
where crabs grow, / And with my long nails will dig thee pignuts, / Show thee a jay's nest . . .' (2.2.164–6) are not merely
descriptive, but also indicate an intimate and native engagement with the land. We never see Prospero or Miranda uttering
such descriptions of the island and it is only from Caliban that
we get a vivid sense of a rich, varied and sensual natural space.
Even the most casual of his comments draws from nature, as
when he asks Stephano and Trinculo to 'tread softly, that the
blind mole may / Not hear a footfall' (4.1.494–5).

Perhaps the most lyrical of Caliban's speeches is also on
the 'qualities o' th' isle'. 'Be not afeard', he tells Trinculo and
Stephano,

> The isle is full of noises,
> Sounds and sweet airs that give delight and hurt not.
> Sometimes a thousand twangling instruments
> Will hum about mine ears; and sometimes voices,
> That if I then had waked after long sleep,
> Will make me sleep again; and then in dreaming,
> The clouds methought, would open, and show riches
> Ready to drop upon me, that when wak'd
> I cried to dream again.
>
> (3.2.135–43)

Besides refreshing our perspective on the island, making us see
it not simply as a backdrop, but as a living, breathing, space
that is aesthetic and even spiritual, this passage shows that, in
spite of the overwhelming awareness of his master's presence,

Caliban's island lies outside the reach of Prospero's powers. There are times, in Caliban's dreams, that Prospero does not even exist on it and the island operates only for him, Caliban. The 'sounds and sweet airs' that so move him do not seem to be of Prospero's making. The unreal voices and the lyrical instruments that 'hum' about his ears are forces outside all human control that operate independently on this island and they all work upon – and for – Caliban. Yet, Caliban's imagination also plays a role in orchestrating the native sounds of the island. 'Methought, the clouds would open', he says, and in a sense, they do so in his dreams. The repeated references to sleeping and dreaming combined with the soft sibilant sounds and poignant culminating line makes this speech among the most elegant written by Shakespeare. Caliban here is far from being a monster, but is a sensate and feeling being endowed with a finely developed aesthetic sensibility. He too longs for beauty, he too dreams and he too weeps.

Caliban's relationship with language serves to make complex and very relevant points about language and identity, language and subjugation and language and agency. His native tongue, whatever it might have been, has been completely erased. As far as Miranda is concerned, Caliban simply 'gabbled' before he was taught her and Prospero's language. Miranda also reminds him that their language made him human and that before he was introduced to it he was merely 'A thing most brutish' (1.2.358). Ironically, it is his masters' language that makes Caliban the complete and articulating subject (Miranda tells him that she 'endowed thy purposes / With words that made them known' (1.2.358–9)), even as it is the very same 'gift' of language that further inscribes him as their servant. Conversely, if Prospero and Miranda thought that Caliban's servility would be further ensured if he spoke like they did, he proves them wrong. In lines that are among the most famous in the play, he defiantly says, 'You taught me language, and my profit on't / Is I know how to curse' (1.2.364–5). Language becomes his most powerful – and only – weapon against his oppressors. In spite of the effacement of his native language, language still allows Caliban to evoke his mother and to protest the wrongs done to him. The play thus unexpectedly produces sites of resistance against power even as it makes Prospero's power out to be all encompassing. Language is one such site, and this makes us aware of how language operates as discourse – it functions in social contexts, is impacted by them, even as it shapes and remakes them.

The play also stages Caliban planning and attempting to execute a revolution. Trinculo stumbles upon him and wonders what 'strange fish' he has found (2.2.27). The sailor's first impulse is dictated by greed as he wonders if he can transport this strange being to England to exhibit, just as American natives were brought back and displayed in public for a fee. In turn, Caliban reacts to Trinculo as if the man was a god. 'Has thou not dropped from heaven?' he asks in wonder (2.2.134). Here, the reader sees little of the proud, defiant Caliban of the earlier scene. Instead, he is reduced to a grovelling slave who mistakes the two drunken wastrels for deities. He is indeed a 'poor credulous monster' (2.2.143) as Trinculo puts it. Aristotle's theory that some men are natural slaves and that servitude is an inborn, inherited state of mind (a theory that was revived in the Renaissance) seems to be reinforced by the Caliban we see here. He needs little more than a little liquor to enslave him. Rebellions in Shakespeare are often turned into comic episodes and we see the planned revolt in *The Tempest* going the same way. Caliban's behaviour is both humorous and pathetic. He repeats the very same, self-destructive pattern of behaviour as he did when Prospero landed on the island. He will show this second set of newcomers the best springs and fetch berries, fish and wood for them, as he did for Prospero. Even Trinculo is a little startled at this unexpected adulation and exclaims at this 'most ridiculous monster – to make a wonder of a poor drunkard' (2.2.162–3). Caliban's song at the end of the first scene talks of a life without labour and ends with a ringing cry of freedom 'Freedom, high-day; high-day freedom; freedom high-day, freedom'

(2.2.181–2). But then the very same song also celebrates the fact that he 'Has a new master, (2.2.180). Caliban is caught between the desire for liberty and a dependence on servitude, and his language consistently reflects this paradox.

In the next scene with Stephano and Trinculo, Caliban attempts to narrate his story. He begins clearly enough, 'As I told thee before, I am subject to a tyrant, / A sorcerer, that by his cunning hath / Cheated me of the island' (3.2.40–2), but the attempt to recount this past is turned into a farce with Ariel's interruptions, and quarrels erupting between Trinculo and Caliban. Even Caliban's 'the isle is full of noises speech' is wasted on his new 'friends'. Under certain circumstances, language seems to be as pointless as it is powerful in others.

In contrast to this poetic speech is Caliban's other piece of extended dialogue. He plans the party's encounter with Prospero:

> thou mayst brain him,
> Having first seized his books, or with a log
> Batter his skull, or paunch him with a stake,
> Or cut his wezand with thy knife. Remember
> First to possess his book, for without them
> He's but a sot, as I am, nor hath not
> One spirit to command. They all do hate him
> As rootedly as I. Burn but his books.
>
> (3.2.88–95)

The speech is articulate and impassioned, but to gory effect. The images of violence are startling and excessive. Both Caliban the clown and Caliban the poet are replaced by a vicious, bloodthirsty creature. Caliban's strategy is simple and crude though his recognition of the connection between Prospero's power and his knowledge is a sophisticated one. The forceful alliteration in his plea to 'Burn but his books', highlights the terrible beauty of violence, as perceived by Caliban. Besides, the speech is dominated by imperative constructions ('Batter his skull', 'Burn but his books'). Imperatives are interesting because they can be both commands and pleas. Is Caliban grovelling before the two sailors here, begging them to execute his vision, or does the immense passion of his hatred for Prospero make Caliban take charge and command and instruct, in spite of his reliance on the others? These lines leave room for actors' and readers' interpretation.

When they actually come to as close as they ever would to executing the scheme to overthrow Prospero, Trinculo and Stephano are drunk and distracted. But there is a discernable change in Caliban's demeanour here. He alternatively cajoles them: 'Be patient' (4.1.205) and flatters them: 'Prithee, my king, be quiet . . . and I, thy Caliban, / For aye thy footlicker' (4.1.215, 218–19), but he is clearly no longer in awe of the two drunks. When they stop to gawk at the 'shining apparel' Ariel has hung out to distract them, Caliban refuses to be diverted and mutters his impatience 'The dropsy drown this fool! What do you mean / To dote thus on such luggage? Let't alone / And do the murder first' (4.1.231–3). The drunkards' antics not only serve to trivialize the entire rebellion, but also serve, by contrast, to highlight Caliban's superiority to them. This, along with his sense of urgency and purpose, invests him with a certain dignity. He is no longer the bumbling clown or the servile footlicker of the earlier scenes. But it is quite clear to the audience right from the start that his project is doomed to failure. We would laugh at Caliban's foolish optimism, but as Peter Hulme writes, 'the poignancy of his position should surely sour any possible laughter'.

The last act sees Caliban and party driven into stage by Ariel. The other characters in the play are drawn together in solidarity and it is quite clear that these three, especially Caliban, will never be one of them. Stephano and Trinculo are blustering, and ridiculous in their stolen clothing. Caliban is simply frightened. 'I'm afraid / He [Prospero] will chastise me', he says (5.1.262–3). He is greeted with laughter by the Italian party, even by Sebastian and Antonio, who have their own misdemeanours to repent. Prospero tells Alonso that he must 'know and own' Stephano and Trinculo (5.1.275); as for Caliban, 'this thing of darkness I / Acknowledge mine' (5.1.275–6). 'Acknowledge' is a puzzling choice of word and has incited much critical debate. On the one hand, Prospero might be simply asserting his ownership of Caliban. On the other hand, he could be admitting his responsibility for him, ruefully recognizing that he has played a part in making Caliban the discontent, violent, frightened 'thing of darkness' that he has become. It could indeed be a moment where Prospero is acknowledging the darkness in him, the fact that Caliban is not completely and absolutely outside or in opposition to him. In any case, the word signals the moment of greatest intimacy between Prospero and Caliban, the intense and infinitely complicated nature of the master's feelings towards his slave, or the colonizer's towards the colonized, or simply a man's towards his enemy.

Caliban for his part slinks away with a resolution to be 'wise hereafter / And seek for grace' (295–6). He repents for his transgressions and he seeks Prospero's mercy and forgiveness. But once again, the reader has questions: How real is Caliban's remorse? And how long will it last? Is this merely a temporary truce? Prospero might not have affected any real change as far as Antonio and Sebastian are concerned. Has he been successful with Caliban? In the tradition of comedy, Caliban, the villain and the outsider, is not only not part of the final communal celebration, but he also remains a puzzle to the end. It also remains unclear if Caliban will stay in the island or whether he will go back to Milan, a slave forever. As we will see in Chapter 3, more than any other Shakespearean character, Caliban has fascinated and moved writers and artists the world over, who have identified their own political predicaments in him, and who have consequently imagined his future for him in various ways. In spite of the shifting representations of this monster, what has stayed with these and other writers is Caliban's exuberant call for freedom and his need to dream again.

## *Writing women – Sycorax and Miranda*

Caliban's mother Sycorax is all the history and heritage that he can claim. She remains a shadowy figure, however, whose story we know only through Prospero, who certainly has reason to be biased against her. Marina Warner writes that 'among the noises of the isle, the voice of Sycorax is silenced. Her story is evoked in a few scant lines that do not flesh out a full character or even tell a coherent tale; in fragments, like the shiftings of an archaeological dig, her past is glimpsed only to fade again'.

The language used by Prospero to describe Sycorax is among the most vivid and unusual in the play. She is not only a 'foul witch', but also is, with 'age and envy' 'grown into a hoop' (1.2.258, 59), indicating a state of moral and physical deformity that is more startling and extreme than anything said about Caliban. She is also a 'blue-eyed hag' (1.2.269), a description that has never failed to puzzle. The colour of her eyes challenges our idea of what a North African witch ought to look like, and some scholars have concluded that blue eyelids might not be used here as a marker of racial identity, but might have denoted pregnancy during the Renaissance. The 'one thing' that Sycorax is said to have done for which she could not be killed (1.2.266) is also perplexing, and might, once again, refer to her pregnancy which resulted in her escaping execution (according to the laws of the time, pregnant female convicts could not be killed). Instead, Sycorax is banished to the island where she 'litters' her child Caliban. In contrast to Miranda who exemplifies chastity and virtue, Sycorax's deviant sexuality evokes the other, darker, side of the feminine.

A pregnant, blue-eyed Algerian witch exiled on an island is quite a creation, even if it comes from Shakespeare's fertile imagination. By virtue of the fact that she is both a witch and foreigner, Sycorax becomes doubly an outsider. Her knowledge of magic is especially interesting given Prospero's own status as magus. As a female magician, Sycorax is associated with Circe, Medea and other mythological women who practiced the dark arts, even as she invokes the home-grown witch who was an immediate and threatening reality to Renaissance readers. Sycorax's magic is depicted as dark and malignant. She practices 'mischiefs manifold and sorceries terrible' (1.2.264), she forces the 'delicate' spirit Ariel to 'act her earthy and abhorred commands' (1.2.273) and when he dares to disobey, she 'in her most unmitigable rage' (1.2.276) imprisons him in a cloven pine. Even as she is not an active presence in the play, Sycorax is necessary to make Prospero the text's moral centre. Her magic, black, female, and now obsolete, serves to highlight Prospero's magic, which is white, male and, ultimately, more dynamic.

However, as discussed earlier, the nature of Prospero's magic is questionable. His description of Sycorax's ability to 'control the moon, make flows and ebbs' (5.1.270) is reminiscent of Prospero's own ability to dim the sun and call forth winds. There might be more of an affiliation between Sycorax and Prospero than he cares to admit to. He is also, like her, a reluctant exile and the single parent of an only child. In fact, although he has never met her, she is persistently present in his memory, almost obsessively so. This, as Dympna Callaghan, argues, bears all the characteristics of what has been termed 'colonial desire'. Racial difference was perceived as crucial in the context of colonialism, but the very construction of this difference 'simultaneously prohibits and provokes erotic contact with the other'. The language that Prospero uses when he speaks of Sycorax indicates his fear, and repulsion, as well as a fascination bordering on desire. All of this renders Sycorax a force that is absent but vivid and intense.

If Sycorax belongs to the past, Miranda is the symbol of the future. Like Caliban, she too has been nurtured on the island. Her name too has been carefully chosen by the playwright from the Latin *mirandus* denoting 'wonderful'. And Ferdinand's response to the unexpected sight of a young girl on what he thought was a deserted island is one of awestruck astonishment. 'O, you wonder!' he exclaims (1.2.427) on seeing her, and later addresses her as 'Admired Miranda! / Indeed

the top of admiration, worth / What's dearest to the world!'
(3.1.37–9). The responses Miranda invokes are reminiscent
of the amazement with which Europeans responded to the
New World with its exotic and unexpected beauty. If Caliban
recalls the strange and frightening new land, Miranda stands
for its lushness, fertility (America was often depicted in erotic
terms as a naked woman) and the seemingly infinite promise
held by the new continents.

Miranda is an unusual figure. She is among the most solitary of Shakespeare's heroines, brought up on an island with
no one but her father, a 'monster' and an airy spirit for company. The memory of the 'four or five women' that attended
on her (1.2.47) is a fading one, and as we saw earlier, Prospero
controls the entire narrative of their pre-island past. 'Obey
and be attentive', he commands (1.2.38), and launches into
her story. Domineering as he is, the language that Prospero
uses with Miranda does not discount the deep tenderness
he feels for her. He addresses her as 'my girl' and 'cherubin'
(1.2.61, 152) and most movingly attributes to her his desire
and ability to stay alive ('Thou wast that did preserve me'
(1.2.153)). Most of his actions in the play are dictated by
the need to secure her happiness and rights. Prospero takes
pride in the fact that even on the island he has provided his
daughter an education befitting her noble birth. He has above
all schooled her to dislike Caliban. Miranda describes him
as a 'villain' whom she does 'not love to look on' (1.2.310–
11). As discussed on page 28, Miranda's angry outburst at
Caliban ('Abhorred slave, / Which any print of goodness wilt
not take' (1.2.352–3)) was assigned by editors to Prospero on
the grounds that not only would bashful little Miranda be
entirely incapable of such a furious denunciation, but it also
would have been indecorous on her part to reply to Caliban's
coarse reference to the attempted rape. Besides, her lines refer
to her teaching Caliban language, something she would surely
have been too young to do when she first landed on the island.
Editors have also defended themselves on the grounds that the
style of the speech, the use of polysyllabic words and the use

of the second person 'thee' is more characteristic of Prospero's speech than Miranda's. Contemporary editors have, however, returned to ascribing this speech to Miranda.

This might seem an inconsequential editorial quibble, but it does indicate that the language of the play allows Miranda to be read in vastly different ways. For those who believe that the 'Abhorred slave' lines simply could not have been hers, Miranda is the naive, young, chaste child of the island who is controlled by a domineering father, and who eventually falls in love with a prince who ships her off to the happily ever after and a sequestered royal life. But the play also holds out the possibility that Miranda is tougher, more sexually aware and quite able to speak for herself. Her angry outburst to Caliban is not only natural, but also called for at that moment. What young woman wouldn't speak up at such provocation? Besides, it could be argued Miranda is after all no longer a child, has grown up on an island with a young male (even if he is perceived as more monstrous than human) and things of nature, and would surely be more sexually aware than her father (or readers) think or want her to be.

We catch another glimpse of the somewhat more assertive Miranda in her interactions with Ferdinand. She insistently pleads with her father on the young stranger's behalf in spite of Prospero's angry and pejorative rebukes ('What, I say, / My foot my tutor?' and 'Silence! One word more / Shall make me chide thee, if not hate thee' (1.2.469–70, 476–7)). She later disobeys her father's explicit command and reveals her name to Ferdinand and speaks to him at length though she is aware that 'I prattle, / Something too wildly, and my father's precepts / I therein do forget' (3.1.57–9). Prospero has set himself up as the guardian of her chastity, not only safeguarding it from Caliban, but also repeatedly threatening Ferdinand with the most dire of consequences if he dares to 'break her virgin-knot' (4.1.15) before the necessary marriage ceremonies. The restrictions imposed by her father seem to irk Miranda and she weeps in irritation 'At mine own unworthiness that dare not offer / What I desire to give, and much less take / What I shall die to want' (3.1.77–79). It is possible therefore to see Miranda both as the subdued female whose body constitutes the ground over which Caliban and Prospero battle, and whose beauty and promised fertility are the means her father uses to regain his place in Italian society, as well as a desiring, speaking woman, who is more self-assured, even forceful, than apparent at first.

Shakespeare's romantic heroines usually turn out to be interesting and complicated figures in unique and individual ways, but they all always find happiness in marriage at the end of the comedies. In the tradition of romance, the fitting climax to the plot is Prospero promising Alonso yet another 'wonder to content ye / As much as me my dukedom' (5.1.170–71) and then dramatically revealing Ferdinand and Miranda, alive, together and playing chess. The young people are rather unexpectedly quarrelling over their game at this moment with Miranda telling her 'Sweet Lord' that 'you play me false' (5.1.172), but perhaps one should not read too much into that. It is a playful wrangling, and Shakespeare has nicely rewritten chess, that game symbolizing war, as the pastime of lovers. However, the same uncertainty that hangs over Caliban's future hovers over Miranda's as well, though perhaps to lesser extent. She is going back to Italy but the world of the royal court is going to be foreign to this child of the island. While scholars such as Stephen Orgel argue that *The Tempest* moves towards marriage as all courtship comedy does, 'yet the relations it postulates between men and women are ignorant a best, characteristically tense and potentially tragic'; it is up to individual readers to decide which way to be directed by the language of the play as far as Miranda's happiness is concerned.

Miranda's last lines in the play have resonated with readers. She sees Alonso and his party, her first large group of humans, and exclaims: 'O brave new world / That has such people in't ' (5.1.183–4). The fact that the 'goodly creatures' (5.1.182) include the likes of Antonio makes us unsure of how to receive the lines. Prospero's response – ''Tis new to thee'

(5.1.184) is ambiguous too. It can be read as cynical (where Miranda sees potential and beauty, he sees moral depravity), as ironically tolerant of her naiveté, or as simply weary. He cannot share her exuberance or her innocence. But though the celebrations of tragicomedy are never absolute and undiluted, and though the potential for future sorrow is ever-present, Miranda's comment and the hopefulness and excitement that provokes it are almost necessary. In a play that is constantly aware of the illusory nature of life, loyalty and happiness, at least some of the characters need to believe that love and joy are real and substantial and not merely deceptive fantasies. Miranda possibly stands for the human need to wonder and to hope for better things.

The language of the play, beautiful and profound as it is, continues to provoke questions right up to its conclusion. *The Tempest* does end with the traditional celebration of community with Prospero surrounded by friends and family. Ariel sings an exuberant song of freedom, Miranda finds love and magic has served to establish order and happiness. But even the most joyous of celebrations is informed by the possibility of sorrow. And there are still questions: Has Prospero's project of reform failed with Antonio and Sebastian, who don't utter a word of penitence or apology right to the end? Has it fully succeeded even with Caliban? Has Prospero really changed, and is his resolution to drown his book a real renunciation of power? But even if the aristocrats, for the most part, are united at the end and the more humble born (Stephano and Trinculo) and the outsider (Caliban) become the butt of their ridicule, is there uneasiness in their laughter, and in ours?

The play refuses to give singular or clear-cut answers. It offers and withdraws the possibility of simple interpretation, and puts multiple perspectives and conflicting voices in conversation with each other. This can admittedly be potentially confusing to the reader, but it is the very ambiguity of the language and its continued reliance on paradox, its tendency to juxtapose irreconcilable tones and diction that encourage divergent readings. This is what makes reading *The Tempest* a pleasurable experience and writing about it an interesting and fulfilling project.

# Writing matters

Your final writing project on *The Tempest* is likely to be a critical essay. However, any good critical essay, whatever its focus, builds on the detailed analysis of individual passages. In this chapter, we selected some of these passages and examined them, usually to point out their ambiguity and to alert ourselves to the multiple and often contradictory meanings the play communicates. As someone writing on *The Tempest*, you will find yourself doing similar work.

*Close reading* or *explication* is the technical term used to describe the task of examining, in great detail, the words, figures of speech and structure of a passage, piece of dialogue or scene. The technique is based on the assumption that there is a relationship between the form of a literary work and its content – how something is said has a great deal to do with what is being said. It is also based on the assumption that the effect and meaning communicated by the play as a whole is the sum of its parts. It is therefore necessary to confront individual portions of the play, both to make meaning clear and to understand how the work done by the individual scene or speech contributes to the themes and emotional effect of the entire play. While it is not always difficult to make vague, generalized statements about the play ('*The Tempest* is the most complex of Shakespeare's plays', '*The Tempest* is neither a tragedy nor a comedy, it is a blend of the two', 'Caliban is the real hero of *The Tempest*, while Prospero is the antagonist', etc.), these statements need to be grounded in the explication of individual passages.

Begin by choosing the passage you wish to explicate. Try not to choose entire scenes (unless they are very brief). Focus instead on a relatively brief exchange between two characters or a speech by any one character. Read the passage a number of times, keeping in mind that you simply cannot close read unless you comprehend the meaning of every word and phrase in the passage. So use the footnotes or look up words in a dictionary. It is often useful to consult the footnotes and/or a dictionary even if you do know the meaning of the word, as you might be alerted to additional connotations and associations. You don't need to write about every word or even every line in the passage you choose. Simply focus on what you think are the features that stand out. Begin by writing down your argument about the passage, follow it up with the explication and conclude with a brief statement that shows how this particular passage throws light on the work as a whole. You need to convince your reader that the passage you have chosen is important enough to comment on.

For example, on page 34 of this chapter, we looked closely at the language used in the scene in which the court party reacts to the island. Our argument about this passage could be stated as, '*The island in "The Tempest" is represented in contradictory terms. It represents refuge and deliverance even as it stands for sterility and despair.*' This statement is followed up with a close analysis of the language of the scene. We looked at the adjectives used by the various characters and at how opposing descriptive terms are placed against each other ('air breathes sweetly' – 'rotten' lungs, 'lush and lusty' grass – 'tawny' grass), emphasizing the contradictory representation of the island. We also commented on the tones used by the speakers: Gonzalo's hopefulness and excitement as opposed to Antonio's sneering cynicism. In an even more detailed analysis, we could also have looked at the order of presentation: while both the optimists and the cynics get equal space, the exchange does end with Gonzalo's hopeful assertion. This might be significant. We could also have examined sentence structure: Gonzalo's exclamatory sentences which could come across as naive and high pitched *or* as poetic and exalted and Antonio's flat and relatively brief declaratives, which could read as to the point and commonsensical or as dull and indicating a refusal to really engage with the landscape. Our concluding statement could be something like this: '*These contradictory descriptions of the island are indicative of the world-view of "The Tempest" as a whole, which also moves between hope and cynicism regarding humans, their achievements and potential for goodness.*' You could also use this passage to point out that opposition and contradiction are central to the language of the play and consider how this impacts readers. Does it leave them bewildered and confused? Does it complicate their response to the play in some profound and productive way?

In addition to the scenes we have focused on in this chapter, the sections in which Ariel appears offer more opportunities to practice detailed analysis. Ariel's first entrance is in the second scene of the opening act.

> Prospero: Come away, servant, come; I am ready now
>     Approach, my Ariel. Come.
>
> *(Enter* ARIEL)
>
> Ariel: All hail, great master; grave sir, hail! I come
>     To answer thy best pleasure, be't to fly,
>     To swim, to dive into the fire, to ride
>     On the curled clouds. To thy strong, task
>     Ariel and all his quality.
>
> (1.2.189–93)

Begin with this and read the next 100-odd lines where Ariel and Prospero converse with each other. Some things to focus on as you attempt a detailed analysis of this portion of the scene are as follows:

- How does Ariel address Prospero? Comment on the terms of address he uses.

- Note the variety of terms Prospero uses to address and describe Ariel. What do you think they tell us about his feelings towards Ariel?

● What or who is Ariel? Note the description of his dart-ing around as fire and flame on the ship, his charming the mariners to sleep. Why are there so many verbs in these passages?

● Take note of Ariel's numerous disguises. How do you imagine Ariel? Where does the language of the play direct you in this regard?

● When the invisible Ariel addresses the courtiers, his tone changes completely – he becomes the voice of revenge and judgment. Look carefully at these lines and consider whether Shakespeare simply has Ariel speaking for Prospero here. In other words, is this Prospero speaking in another guise, or is Ariel's lan-guage unique, differing from his master's?

● Ariel was Sycorax's servant, was freed by Prospero, who paradoxically demands servitude in return for liberty. How does Ariel connect to the larger themes of liberty and bondage in the play?

You can do similar work with the other passages where Ariel appears, ending with the famous song envisioning liberty, 'Where the bee sucks . . .' (5.1.88–94).

*The Tempest* is full of passages and brief scenes that lend themselves to detailed analysis. You can select any number of them, always remembering in your response to make a point or have an argument about the passage and also pointing out why the particular passage you have chosen is important to the play as a whole.

A *comparison and contrast* exercise also gives you the opportunity to analyse two different (but relatively short) passages in detail. For example, Caliban and Ariel have inter-esting similarities as well as differences. You could compare the scenes in which Prospero addresses each of them, or the short songs ('No more dams . . .' (2.2.176–80) and 'Where the bee sucks') in which each of the two servants visualizes his freedom. When you engage in a comparison–contrast writing exercise make sure of the following:

- Clarify what you want to accomplish in the exercise. Is it to throw light on both Caliban and Ariel (in this particular example)? Or to emphasize and understand one of the characters and use the other only as a point of similarity or contrast?

- You also need to be sure there is a reason to compare two passages. There might be good reason to compare passages involving Caliban and Ariel (think of why this is the case). What about Ferdinand and Caliban? Miranda and Caliban? Antonio and Gonzalo? Alonso and Prospero? Milan and the island? Select and analyse passages involving one or more of the pairs suggested here.

# CHAPTER TWO

# Language: Forms and uses

Even the casual reader of *The Tempest* will notice right away that that the language of the play is incredibly beautiful and opaque. When one talks of the 'opacity' of the language of literature one is referring less to its difficulty than to the fact that it is not merely a vehicle for meaning, that is, it does not simply serve to signify objects or to communicate ideas, thoughts and feelings. This kind of language also draws attention to itself; it invites, even forces, the reader to notice it for its own sake. Besides, whatever the philosophical, political and other meanings conveyed by a piece of literature, the beauty, possibilities, as well as the limitations and even dangers of language, are always being explored by the literary artist. In other words, language is any writer's inevitable and natural theme.

Shakespeare sometimes overtly ponders the efficacy and purpose of language. 'To what end are all these words?' he asks in *The Taming of the Shrew* (1.2.803). The characters in *The Tempest* sometimes seem more certain of language's tremendous potency. For Miranda, it is an instrument of civilization and means of control over Caliban. 'I endowed thy purposes / With words that made them known' (1.2.358–9), she tells him. Caliban, in turn, appropriates and refashions his masters' language to suit his own purposes. He was taught their language 'and my profit on't / Is I know how to curse' (1.2.364–5). We are also told that Antonio put his base desires into words and was consequently able to realize them ('Who, having into truth by telling of it, / Made such a sinner of his memory / To credit his own lie' (1.2.100–102)). Language then serves in the play as a means of control, an instrument of impassioned protest and a clever means to further one's ambitions. It functions as 'discourse' in that human experience and reality are structured and experienced by and through it.

This awareness of the power of language is discernible through the play. Like other literary texts, *The Tempest* is characterized by what has been described as 'cohesion' or an evident internal patterning by way of the deliberate use of rhyme, metre, repetition, parallel structures and a unified diction. However, in spite of the play's linguistic self-consciousness, literary tropes and other devices are applied subtly and with a very light touch. In Frank Kermode's words, the play's language is 'artificially natural', even as the writer is certainly very aware that a good play is a skilful linguistic performance and sensitive readers, in their turn, know to identify and describe the forms and uses of language in the text and think about how they contribute to the play's theme and overall effect.

## Structure and sound

*The Tempest* is among Shakespeare's shortest plays. It is also among the most perfectly structured. It begins with a shipwreck and people hopelessly scattered around an island and ends with the restoration of the ship and the party happily brought back together, ready to sail home. The classical 'unities' of time and place, which require that the action occurs within a 24-hour period and in one specific location, are carefully observed. The 'unity of action' that requires a single, tightly woven plot is more or less followed as well, in that the Caliban thread of the story is well integrated into the main plot and has many parallels with it (Caliban's rebellion echoes Antonio and Sebastian's plot against Alonso, which in turn recalls Prospero's overthrow in Milan several years ago). The single setting emphasizes the island's symbolic significance and raises questions about attitudes to place, the links between place and identity and place and power, as we discussed in Chapter 1. The play's insistence on the unity of time also has some interesting effects. The fact that the entire action takes place in a few hours not only gives the play a tightness of structure that is pleasingly neat and spare, but it also leaves much unsaid – we remain unsure of Antonio's penitence, Caliban's future, the fate of Claribel and of Sycorax's past. While these silences and loose ends might be unsatisfying to some readers and audiences, they also complicate our understanding of beginnings, endings, poetic justice and plot resolutions.

Like all Shakespeare's plays, *The Tempest* is mostly in unrhymed iambic pentameter, often referred to as 'blank verse'. The 'iamb' is a metrical foot consisting of two syllables, an unaccented or unstressed one (conventionally indicated with a ˘ ) followed by an accented one (conventionally marked with a / ). For example, 'slumber', 'subtle', 'earthly', 'compare' are all iambs. 'Pentameter' is a line of verse consisting of five metrical feet. For example, all of these lines are in pentameter:

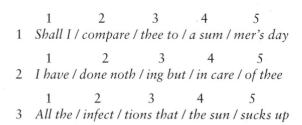

When each foot in a line is an iamb, and there are five iambic feet to the line, we have a line in iambic pentameter. If we consider the lines quoted above, marking the pattern of accented and unaccented syllables, as well as counting the number of feet, we will see that all of them are in iambic pentameter:

˘ / ˘ / ˘ / ˘ / ˘ /
1   *Shall I / compare / thee to / a sum / mer's day*

˘ / ˘ / ˘ / ˘ / ˘ /
2   *I have / done noth / ing but / in care / of thee*

Iambic pentameter was the metre of choice for Shakespeare and other Renaissance poets because it duplicated the rhythms of natural speech and when delivered well has a sonorous and beautiful effect. 'It is not rhyming and versing [alone] that maketh a poet', writes Sidney. Yet, Renaissance writers, including Sidney, recognized that metre and rhyme invested a piece of writing with elegance and beauty (Puttenham comments that 'Poesie is a skill to speake and write harmoniously: and verses or rime be a kind of musical utterance, by reason of a certaine congruitie in sounds pleasing the ear'). Metre also made it easier to remember lines; as Sidney writes, 'verse far exceedeth prose in the knitting up of the memory'. Of course, not all characters in the play speak in blank verse. Trinculo and Stephano, like most low-born and comic characters in Renaissance drama consistently speak in prose. But what is interesting is that Antonio and Sebastian speak in blank verse for the most part, even while discussing their assassination plot. Why does Shakespeare make this choice? Is it only because they are aristocrats, or is it to show that poetry can lend itself to deception and that the masterful use of language can be directed to undesirable ends? It is even more significant that not only is Caliban given some of the most exquisitely lyrical lines in the play, but he also generally speaks in blank verse. The fact that he is endowed with a capacity for poetry invites the reader to reconsider his role as monster and villain.

The use of iambic pentameter as the dominant metre in the play has led to other curious effects. Shakespeare sometimes omits syllables from words in order to adhere to the iambic pentameter. Prospero's speeches in 1.2 are full of such omissions ('in lieu o' th' premises', 'hearts i'th' state' and 'I' th' dead of darkness' are a few examples). He also sometimes omits words from sentences. For example, Prospero says 'there is no soul' (1.2.29) when he means 'there is no soul perished' and 'and his only heir' (1.2.58) when he means 'and you his only heir'. Apart from maintaining the metre, the omissions also invest the verse with a certain compressed quality that hints at the anger and distress fermenting in Prospero, which he cannot fully express. Conversely, Shakespeare often adds an extra unaccented syllable at the end of the blank verse line. Even a brief extract like this one will indicate how Shakespeare does not hesitate to slightly modify the syllabic count of a line:

| | |
|---|---|
| I thus neglecting worldly ends, all dedicated | (13 syllables) |
| To closeness and the bettering of my mind | (11 syllables) |
| With that which, but being so retired, | (10 syllables) |
| O'er prized all popular rate, in my false brother | (13 syllables) |
| Awaked an evil nature, and my trust, | (10 syllables) |
| | (1.2.89–93) |

This profusion of irregular lines in the play in general and this scene in particular, either because of omission or addition, needs to be noted. 'Literariness' is characterized by both order and disorder. While metre orders the language into a pattern and therefore creates an order that is pleasing, too much order is ineffective. The reader or listener's perception becomes automated and it ceases to please or to provoke. As Shklovsky writes, art is characterized by 'a disordering which cannot be predicted'. In the case of this scene, the irregular lines invite attention because they occur against the ordered pattern of the iambic pentameter and add to the feeling of agitation and perturbation. However, there is still a sense of order, unity and interconnection because of the repetition of sounds through the use of alliteration, or the repetition of the same consonant sounds at the beginnings of nearby words ('O'er-prized all popular rate' (1.2.92), 'to my state grew stranger' (1.2.76), 'Subject his coronet to his crown' (1.2.114) and 'i' th' dead of darkness' (1.2.130) to quote a few examples), consonance, or the repetition of the same consonant sounds in the middle of words ('neglecting worldly ends' (1.2.89)) and assonance, or the repetition of the same vowels sounds in nearby words ('for thou must now know further' (1.2.33), a 'freckled whelp' (1.2.283)) along with a profusion of the repetition of complete words ('O, I have suffered / With those that I saw suffer –' (1.2.5–6), 'I have done nothing but in care of thee, / Of thee, my dear one, thee my daughter' (1.2.16–17), 'Both, both, my girl' (1.2.61)). This repetition invests the writing with a rhythmic incantatory quality. The combining of the irregular with the unified and interlinked, enacts, at the level of sound, what Alden and Virginia Vaughan describe as 'the plot's underlying tension between harmony and disruption, between utopian longings and the chaos caused by human nature'.

# Diction

Diction refers to a writer's word choices, or more generally, to the type of language used in a literary text. It is well known that not only did Shakespeare possess an immensely wide, varied and rich vocabulary, but that he has also further enhanced the language by introducing his own neologisms or coinages. *The Tempest* is noted for the use of a large number of original compound words. These include (among several others) 'wide-chopped', 'spell-stopped', 'cloud-capped', 'hag-born', 'pole-clipt', 'never-surfeited' and 'sea-change'. Once again, meanings that would normally be conveyed in one or more sentences are collapsed, adding to the sense of compression discussed earlier.

The play is also characterized by the recurrence of certain words through the text. The word 'delicate' is one such example. Prospero describes Ariel as a 'a spirit too delicate'

(1.2.272) to perform Sycorax's commands. This description gives the sense of a sensitive and somewhat frail being who has been brutally treated and needs Prospero to be his saviour. The adjective is once again associated with Ariel when Prospero says 'Delicate Ariel, / I'll set thee free for this' (1.2.442–3). By this point in the narrative, Ariel has proved himself to be far from fragile or weak – here, the word 'delicate' serves to convey Prospero's affection, even admiration, for this fine, lovely, strange creature who has been his servant. The word is used again by Adrian with reference to the island's 'subtle, tender and delicate temperance' (2.1.44–5). However, Adrian is being sarcastic here as made clear by Antonio who recasts the word to slightly bawdy effect and retorts, 'Temperance was a delicate wench' (2.1.46). The word 'delicate' is finally used by Stephano when he stumbles upon Caliban: 'Four legs and two voices – a most delicate monster!' (2.2.88–9). Here, Prospero's description of Ariel is parodied and that same word is used to incongruous effect. Caliban is the antithesis of Ariel and the adjective 'delicate' used for both characters sets them apart, even as it might hint at continuities between two beings, neither of whom are human and both of who are Prospero's servants.

Similarly, the word 'strange' can also be traced through the play. Prospero's enemies have landed on the island 'By accidents most strange' (1.2.179), Alonso wonders 'what strange fish' might have swallowed his son (2.1.113), Trinculo thinks Caliban is 'A strange fish' (2.2.27), 'Solemn and strange music' (3.3) is heard through the island by the shipwrecked group and 'strange shapes' (3.3) appear and disappear. Towards the end of the play Alonso remarks, 'These are not natural events; they strengthen / From strange to stranger' (5.1.227–28). The word recurs several more times in the play and encompasses a range of meanings – unnatural, unreal, bewildering – and each use impacts the meaning of subsequent occurrences. Variations of the word 'strange' ('monstrous', 'wondrous', 'divine') are also scattered through the play, and discovering, understanding, and either coming to terms with or rejecting the strange, the unusual and the unexpected becomes an important feature of the narrative. While the frequent repetition of a word is usually frowned upon as it seems to indicate a limited vocabulary, Shakespeare defies the rule to good effect. These recurrences serve to unify the play and also give us a sense of the variety and depth of meaning carried by a single word. Just like the characters in the play, there is more to things than obvious at first glance. The reader can discern other similar lexical patterns through the play. They collectively do the work of tying the play's diction together, creating a certain mood and emphasizing certain themes.

Specific kinds of rhetoric can be discerned through the text. The very opening act figures the panicky sailors' colourful curses and, more significantly, both Prospero and Caliban engage in cursing and countercursing each other. On his very first appearance, Caliban wishes that 'A southwest blow on ye / And blister you all o'er' (1.2.324–5) and Prospero curses back, 'For this, be sure, tonight thou shalt have cramps, / Side-stitches, that shall pen thy breath up' (1.2.326–7) and so forth. The play continues to be scattered with master's and slave's curses. The curse is an interesting use of performative language in that language actually *does* (or is meant to accomplish) something. It brings about and shapes the course of reality. In the play, Prospero's curses have truly material effects and are a sign of his power while Caliban's are a sign of his frustration and relative powerlessness, though as he also says, it is his knowledge of language that teaches him to curse. The language of curse is countered and eventually balanced by the language of prayer. In Act 1, Miranda out of the compassion in her 'piteous heart' (1.2.14) pleads with her father for the men she fears are drowning. And the play ends with Prospero, who might have also learned the lessons of compassion and humility, turning to prayer. Both the cursing and praying indicate a belief in the power of words to alter the course of reality, and the fact that a prayer serves to frame the play at both ends seems to imply a need to believe in its superior authority and strength.

The frequent use of humorous language makes it difficult to define the mood of the play. Shakespeare defied the sticklers for generic purity and easily mingled clowns and kings, humour and high seriousness, even in the most intensely tragic of his plays. Prospero is, however, possibly among the most solemn of Shakespeare's protagonists. It would be hard to imagine him cracking a joke. But humour does occur in unexpected places in the play. While the opening storm scene is commended for its spectacular effect, what's often overlooked is that the writer reworks the storm motif to comic purpose. In an age when artificially-created sound and lighting were very limited, Shakespeare was taking a risk by choosing to start his play with a storm. After the opening stage direction 'a tempestuous noise of thunder and lightning'(1.1), there is actually very little descriptive language to evoke the storm. Instead readers are presented with the sharp and witty exchange between the boatswain and the aristocrats on board. This diverts viewers' attention from what might have been woefully inadequate special effects. However, the humour also serves to highlight some of the themes of the play. The boatswain is irritated by the nobility who are panicking and quite ineffectual in this moment of crisis. His witty irreverence seems completely acceptable at the moment and prepares the reader for the play's complex and shifting treatment of social hierarchies and class distinction. Later in the play too, we wonder if Antonio and others deserve the titles they bear. In another instance of humour in this opening scene, although Gonzalo's wry jokes on the boatswain being destined to die by the gallows rather than at sea and his likening the leaky ship to an 'unstanched wench' (1.1.47) might seem misplaced in this moment of grave danger, they do draw attention to the old councillor's ability to look on things from an ironic distance and with a certain cheerful calm that sets him apart from almost everyone in the play. In a play in which the protagonist eventually recognizes the transience of all things, Gonzalo's humour in the face of the devastating storm is perhaps very much in place.

But there is a certain brand of humorous language that signals less desirable character traits. As the shipwrecked party wanders the island, Antonio and Sebastian engage in a quick and witty exchange that relies largely on puns for humorous effect. Most of their jokes are directed at the gentle Gonzalo. In this case, the ability to be funny is viewed with some disapproval and even suspicion. The two men's ability to twist words and meanings gestures towards their manipulative and deceptive personalities. They are consistently portrayed as partners in wit and jesting, just as they are partners in crime. Even towards the end of the play when Sebastian and Antonio are being suitably chastised for their wrong doings, the former cannot resist a snigger and quick joke to his friend when Caliban and company are driven onto stage.

The most obvious and perhaps most successful use of humorous language is in the case of Trinculo and Stephano. Like other Shakespearean clowns, these two men also belong to the lower classes. Their humour, always delivered in prose rather than blank verse, is drunken, direct and unselfconscious, as opposed to Antonio and Sebastian's clever, biting wit. Shakespeare rarely stages political revolt led by the commoners and when he does so it is often to comic effect. This serves to play down or erase the intense drama and high passion behind such political movements and to diffuse the threat they posed to the prevailing social order. In *The Tempest* too, the rebels are depicted as bumbling clowns. Sebastian and Trinculo are so ridiculous and comic that the reader does not believe for a minute that their badly conceived plan will succeed. The tension and urgency of the scenes in which Caliban plots Prospero's downfall with them is constantly dispelled, first by Ariel's cheekily comic interruptions (in 3.2) and eventually by Stephano and Trinculo's ridiculous display of childish greed (in 4.1). But, as always in the case of Caliban, we are unsure of how to respond to the unintentional comedy he brings to these scenes. We laugh when he takes Stephano for one of Prospero's spirits and is panic-stricken, and eventually when he decides the two men are gods and grovels before them. However, Caliban is more pathetic than comic, and though the absurdity of his behaviour is hard to ignore in these scenes, we are as likely to be moved to pity as to laughter.

*The Tempest* is perhaps not among Shakespeare's funniest plays, but the instances of humour (along with other features discussed in the introductory chapter) earn it a place among the comedies. More clearly, the fact that humour accompanies villainy in some cases, and that the lines between comedy and pathos are occasionally finely drawn in others, makes it among Shakespeare's most successful tragicomedy.

## Imagery

The air of rich sensuality that characterizes *The Tempest* is due to the extensive use of images to evoke a specific sensory experience. The term 'objective correlative' first popularized by the modernist poet T. S. Eliot is a useful one to understand the purpose that images serve in a literary text. Eliot writes: 'The only way of expressing emotion in the form of art is by finding an "objective correlative"; in other words, a set of objects, a situation, a chain of events which shall be the formula of that particular emotion; such that when the external facts, which must terminate in sensory experience, are given, the emotion is immediately evoked.' In other words, an 'objective correlative' is an image or a pattern of images that together suggest a certain emotional or psychological state. Explicit statements regarding the emotional states of characters in a literary text often mean the writer has to resort to abstractions (*evil*, *good*, *joyous*, *angry*, *bored*, etc.), which in turn leave the reader unconvinced or unmoved. An image, however, serves to make the emotion or idea real and immediate. A successful image makes readers sense and feel the emotion or state of mind for themselves.

While Prospero's language is slightly more complex and abstract – a diction that is perhaps characteristic of the intellectual and philosopher, he too occasionally turns to imagery. The boat on which Prospero fled Milan is described as 'A rotten carcass of a butt, not rigged, / Nor tackle, sail, nor mast – the very rats / Instinctively have quit it' (1.2.146–8). This economic but intense description highlights the drama and terror of that journey to nowhere. Caliban's language is nearly always replete with imagery drawn from his physical experience of his surroundings. As noted on page 32, his descriptions of the island not only bring the setting to life in vivid and vibrant detail, but also indicate a degree of intimacy with the land that is not experienced by any of the other inhabitants of the island. Other visual images are equally powerful. Ariel's description of the havoc he created on the ship is a piece of beautiful and unusual writing:

> Now in the waist, the deck, in every cabin
> I flamed amazement. Sometime I'd divide
> And burn in many places – on the topmast,
> The yards and bowsprit would I flame distinctly,
> Then meet and join.
>
> (1.2.197–201)

The unreal and fantastic is described with an incredible specificity of detail. The passage conveys the rapidity of Ariel's movement from one part of the ship to the other, a speed that would be bewildering and beautiful to the astonished crew. 'I flamed amazement' is a wonderful way to convey Ariel's transfiguration into light and fire, as well as to communicate the shock and awe kindled in his viewers. The entire description might, in fact, be inspired by a fairly lengthy and detailed account of the natural phenomenon usually referred to as 'St. Elmo's Fire' that appears in Strachey's 'True Repertory' and creates in the reader an appreciation of the mystery and magic of the sea, sky and weather. Other descriptions of meteorological phenomenon are equally vivid. The storm-tossed waters are described as 'foaming brine' (1.2.211) and the sky 'would pour down stinking pitch' (1.2.3).

The visual spectacles are particularly powerful and grand because they are conjured up by Prospero's magic. Indeed, this power realizes itself by tapping into the human taste for the visual. Apart from the 'special effects' created at sea, the opulent masque, the mysterious banquets that appear and disappear and the 'glistering apparel' that hangs off trees to seduce Caliban and company are primarily visual in their appeal (4.1). In contrast to the grandeur of these spectacles, is Sycorax's sinister deformation, also described in visual terms: 'The foul witch Sycorax, who with age and envy / Was grown into a hoop' (1.1.258–9). While the description of the withered, bent witch is fairly typical, the use of the word 'hoop' coupled with the implication that the change was long, slow, but inevitable, conveys Prospero's repugnance at the unnaturalness and immorality of the alteration.

It is also interesting to think about what Shakespeare could potentially have described in great detail but refrained from doing. While there are a plethora of words used to describe Caliban ranging from 'tortoise' (1.2.317) to 'fish' (2.2) to 'misshapen knave' (5.1.268) and 'freckled whelp' (1.2.283) – the last conjuring up an unattractive, motley, animal-like creature – there are, in fact, remarkably few specific details, leaving Caliban open to directors' interpretations and readers' wildest imaginations, and also making it possible for readers across the world to identify with him. Again, while all of Shakespearean heroines are beautiful, but rarely extensively described, one or two details regarding their appearance are sometimes included (Portia's golden hair, Cleopatra's sultry complexion, Hermia's petite build, Helena's tall stature). In the case of Miranda, we get almost nothing. In the tradition of Petrarchan poetry, she is simply a 'goddess' (1.2.422), a 'precious creature' (3.1.25) and 'So perfect and so peerless, . . . created / Of every creature's best' (3.1.47–8). The reader is left with a vague sense of great, almost unreal beauty and the sense that Miranda too, like so much else on the island, is a splendid magical being.

Despite the emphasis on visuality, it is sound imagery that dominates *The Tempest*. The isle, as Caliban puts it, 'is full of noises'. It is not easy to convey the sensory experience of sound through words and Shakespeare turns all of his linguistic prowess to the purpose. When Miranda talks of the cries of drowning men, the quality of the sound is conveyed through the emotional impact it had on her: 'the cry did knock / Against my very heart!' (1.2.8–9), and when Prospero tells the story of his flight, we are made to hear the sound of the weeping child in the darkness and the sound of the 'sea that roared to us' (1.2.149) and the sighing winds 'whose pity, sighing back again, / Did us but loving wrong' (1.2.150–51). In this case, the auditory imagery lends tension and energy to what could potentially turn into a rather dull account of past history.

The cries of the drowning men find their parallel in another auditory image – that of Ariel's cries from within the cloven pine 'where thou didst vent thy groans / As fast as millwheels strike' (1.2.280–1). The simile draws upon a commonplace and familiar sound – that of the blade of millwheels hitting water – to convey the surreal and horrific. Coleridge writes that a certain kind of poetry succeeds because it renders the unfamiliar familiar, makes the unreal and fantastic seem vivid and present. This is precisely what Shakespeare accomplishes in this description. Most of us don't quite *believe* either in malignant witches or in spirits imprisoned in oak trees, but the diction of these lines makes Sycorax's action and its effects real and immediate. Similarly, the reader suspends disbelief easily and with pleasure when we are made to hear the 'humming, / And that a strange one too' (2.1.318–19) that wakes up Gonzalo. Pathos and sorrow are also conveyed through sound when Caliban describes the isle's noises, the 'Sounds and sweet airs that give delight and hurt not', the 'thousand twangling instruments' that 'hum about mine ears' (3.2.136–8) and the voices that put him to sleep. There is a wealth of aural detail here, some of it specific and concrete (the 'thousand twangling instruments', for instance) and some of it mysteriously and deliciously vague. All of it together creates the sense of a lush and dense soundscape and of a creature whose head is filled with a veritable orchestra of sound. Another striking sound image is when Alonso is made conscious of his past guilt:

> O, it is monstrous, monstrous!
> Methought the billows spoke and told me of it;
> The wind did sing it to me, and the thunder –
> That deep and dreadful organpipe – pronounced
> The name of Prosper.

(3.3.95–9)

In this passage, the sounds of nature are used to convey Alonso's sense of guilt and the terror that accompanies it. Nature itself functions as both conscience and judge that passes verdict through a series of sounds that are both terrifying and beautiful, much like certain Biblical representations of the divine. Interestingly, there is less and less use of sound imagery as the play draws to a close. The ensemble of sights and sounds that has made up the texture of the play converges in the single but resounding sound of Prospero's voice narrating the epilogue, and then silence.

## Figurative language

A figure of speech or trope is a literary device that associates or compares distinct objects. The word 'trope' is derived from the Greek word *tropos* meaning 'a turn'. For the Latin rhetorician Quintilian, figures of speech are what make literary language exceptional and different. The figure is 'any deviation either in thought or expression from the ordinary and simple method of speaking'. When writers use tropes they are turning or manipulating words to make them mean something else; they modify the literal or denotative meaning of words by evoking their connotations or the meanings associated with them. Perhaps the best-known figures of speech are simile and metaphor and Shakespeare exploits both of them to the fullest in his writing. Both simile and metaphor makes comparisons between two different entities. While simile does so more explicitly (with the use of words such as 'like' or 'as'), metaphor uses no connective words and actually equates the two objects being compared. It has been argued that similes and metaphors are fundamental to the ways humans process the world. We don't just describe things in terms of other things, we actually perceive and experience things in terms of knowledge we already possess about other previously encountered objects. As the French poet Arthur Rimbaud puts it, 'I is another' – even our sense of self, of who we are, comes from comparing ourselves to other people and things. Metaphors and similes introduce comparisons that can be unusual and surprising. They make us experience and understand things in new and unexpected ways and the author can evoke a range of meanings and associations because metaphors can be interpreted differently by different readers.

Some of the metaphors in *The Tempest* are used to purely poetic effect. When Prospero first brings Ferdinand before Miranda he tells her to 'advance' (raise) the 'fringed curtains' of her eyes and look at what lies before her (1.2.408). This could simply be a more lyrical way of directing Miranda's gaze towards the young Ferdinand, but the use of the word 'curtains' suggests the theatre and the deliberate and transformative act of viewing a play. The young man becomes a spectacular vision staged by Prospero for his astonished audience consisting of one. No wonder that Miranda responds with 'What is't, a spirit?' (1.2.410).

Shakespeare uses two metaphors for language. When Gonzalo and Antonio's conversations evoke in Alonso painful memories of the past he says, 'You cram these words into mine ears, against / The stomach of my sense' (2.1.107–8) suggesting that their words are being force-fed to him, that words can potentially wound and make ill, just like harmful foods. Shortly after Gonzalo gently reprimands Sebastian for hurting Alonso with his words ('You rub the sore / When you should bring the plaster' (2.1.139–40)), implying that words can heal and administer to emotional wounds as well as exacerbate them. In both these metaphors, words are represented as concrete, physical entities such as food and wounds that have real, material effects (they can feed, make ill, heal and hurt) on listeners. This awareness of the potency of language, casually suggested in these two passing metaphors, permeates the entire play. Language is powerful in its effects and needs to be taken seriously.

Caliban is often described through metaphor. Miranda compares his speech to that of 'a thing most brutish' (1.2.357) and the descriptions of Caliban as a 'whelp' and 'fish' and 'tortoise' associate him with the uncivilized, inhuman and plain ugly. He is also described as 'filth' (1.2.347) and 'earth' (1.2.314) associating him with the base and the grossly material, in contrast to Ariel, who is of the air, the higher element, and to Prospero, who is art and intellect. Nevertheless, it could be said that Caliban's association with the earth and with animals invites a more sympathetic reading. He can be perceived as fundamental (like the earth itself), natural and eternal. West Indian author George Lamming is responding to the inherent ambiguity of these metaphors when he writes: 'Caliban is in his way a kind of Universal. Like the earth he is always there, generous in gifts, inevitable, yet superfluous and dumb. And like the earth which draws attention to age and therefore to the past, he cannot be devoured.' For readers like Lamming, the earth metaphor conveys that Caliban stands for an energy that is primal, pure and long-standing.

Tropes drawn from nature are not reserved for Caliban alone. When Prospero talks of Antonio's past misdeeds he says his brother 'was / The ivy which had hid my princely trunk / And sucked my verdure out on't' (1.2.85–7). Here, Prospero is the stately and healthy tree trunk that is eventually smothered by ivy. The implication is that Antonio's attack on Prospero was not bold and upfront, but insidious and parasitic. The verb 'sucked' suggests the unseemly voracity that provoked Antonio's actions. Miranda, in her turn, is also addressed as a 'worm' by Prospero. As he witnesses her falling in love with Ferdinand he remarks, 'Poor worm, thou art infected' (3.1.32). The comparison of the romantic heroine to a worm might be somewhat startling to a contemporary reader, but it probably suggests an amused and playful tenderness on Prospero's part as he sees his child wide-eyed with admiration and weak-kneed with love. The association of love with disease (suggested by 'infected') was a common one in love poetry of the period, though in this case the disease is less destructive than it is overwhelming and transformative. More troubling to some readers is another metaphor used by Prospero for Miranda. As she pleads with her father to be gentle with Ferdinand and not try him too harshly, Prospero with either genuine or feigned irritation responds with 'What, I say, / My foot my tutor?' (1.2.469–70). Prospero borrows from another commonplace metaphor of the time that likened the family to the body with the father as head. By extension, the daughter Miranda is merely the foot, and Prospero is asserting his patriarchal authority over her. While there is little ambiguity here, the metaphor when read in context could disturb readers. Prospero might or not be a domineering father. The tone he adopts towards his daughter can be perceived as demeaning, while other readers might argue that too much should not be read into the metaphor. Prospero is simply projecting an air of authority while all along he is simply concerned for his daughter's welfare.

Tropes involving the sea abound in the play. The sea is of course an important aspect of the setting and crucial to the movement of the plot, but it is soon transformed from a reality to trope. It is personified and invested with personality and agency. It swallows the dead (1.2.12, 2.1.251), it 'mocks' the survivors' search for their loved ones (3.3.9), is 'incensed' (3.3.74) and requits or avenges past wrong (3.3.71), and, like Prospero himself, it is both punitive and benign ('Though the seas threaten, they are merciful' (5.1.178)). Ariel tells Alonso, Antonio and Sebastian: 'You are three men of sin, whom destiny, / That hath to instrument this lower world / And what is in't, the never-surfeited sea / Hath caused to belch up you' (3.3.53–6). The lines recall the shipwreck, but the very physical verb 'belch' also indicates that the men's sinfulness has rendered them repulsive even to the sea. The sea's act of 'belching' up the men is simultaneously one of purging, purification and punishment. Similarly, when Ariel sings of the dead undergoing a 'sea-change' (1.2.401), the sea is an agent of absolute and complete transformation. In fact, the idea of 'sea-change' or metamorphosis ties the play together thematically: Sycorax has degenerated, but Alonso and party are to be reformed, Ariel will move out of subjugation, Prospero himself will change for the better, even Caliban, perhaps, learns to 'seek for grace'(5.1.296). This theme of transformation and purification is also sustained by the recurrent alchemical metaphors in the play. The word 'tempest' itself connotes purification. As John Mebane points out, it is a term from alchemy that denotes 'a boiling process which removes impurities from base metal which facilitates its transformation into gold'. As the play draws to its end and Prospero is able to visualize his plans coming to fruition, he says that his 'charms crack not' (5.1.2), another alchemical reference to the breaking of the alembic (the vessel in which the chemicals were being distilled) when subject to too much heat. Prospero also continues the alchemical trope when he talks of his enemies' brains 'boiled within thy skull' (5.1.60) and the 'fumes' that cloud their understanding (5.1.67). Transformation, regeneration and reformation, the movement from death to life, sinfulness to virtue, stupidity and obstinacy to 'grace' inform the trajectory of the play.

Other marine metaphors stand out. When Antonio urges Sebastian to assassinate his brother, Sebastian responds by describing himself as 'standing water' (2.1.221) to which Antonio assures him, 'I'll teach you how to flow' (2.1.222). Sebastian in turn replies: 'Do so. To ebb / Hereditary sloth instructs me' (2.1.222–23). In the final act, Prospero remarks that his enemies' 'understanding / Begins to swell, and the approaching tide / Will shortly fill the reasonable shore / That now lies foul and muddy' (5.1.79–82). In the first instance, the rising tide serves as metaphor for dynamic action that is, however, ruled by greed and is dangerous in its effect, while the 'approaching tide' in the second example stands for growing understanding and reason. Both metaphors together illustrate how Shakespeare exploits varied, even opposing associations, of a single vehicle (in this case, the rising tide) to represent contradictory ideas.

Another way of thinking about metaphors in *The Tempest* is to consider who uses them, to what extent and for what purpose. Oddly enough, although Caliban's language is richly poetic he rarely resorts to metaphor or simile. When he says that Prospero's punitive spirits will set on him 'like apes that mow and chatter at me' (2.2.9) and 'like hedgehogs which / Lie tumbling in my barefoot way' (2.2.10–11), we realize that these are not quite similes at all. Similarly, when he describes Stephano and Trinculo as gods, the description is not metaphorical. For Caliban, the drunkards *are* gods, the spirits *are* apes and hedgehogs. The figurative and the real merge in Caliban's world, which is inhabited by both fear and wishful fantasy to an extent that he cannot or need not resort to metaphor at all.

Antonio and Sebastian, however, use tropes easily and nonchalantly. Their comparison of ambition to flowing water discussed earlier (see p. 91), as well as Antonio's reference to Sebastian letting his fortune sleep (2.1.216) illustrate how the two men manipulate language to push their own point of view and further their own ends. In fact, all their conversations are replete with puns and clever, though not particularly profound, metaphors – garments that sit well on the person stand for power, a conscience is a 'kibe' or sore (2.1.277), and their fellow courtiers are like cats that lap milk (2.1.289). As Gonzalo wryly comments, the two men talk so much and so well that they 'would lift the moon out of her sphere' (2.1.183). Unlike other Shakespeare comedies, wit is associated with villainy in *The Tempest* and the dexterous but casual and somewhat superficial manipulation of language is viewed with some suspicion.

Antonio also appropriates an analogy dear to Shakespeare – that of life and the stage. It is a comparison that the dramatist makes in several plays including *Macbeth* and *As You Like It*. As Antonio attempts to persuade Sebastian to assassinate his brother, he tells him that although the ship was wrecked and the men on it nearly drowned it was for a good reason that some of them were 'cast again'(2.1.251). The word 'cast' not only denotes their being cast up on shore and saved, but also has theatrical connotations that are immediately taken up by Antonio:

And by that destiny to perform an act
Wherof what's past is prologue, what to come
In yours and my discharge!

(2.1.252–4)

The course of events directed by destiny and Sebastian's life up till now, Antonio cleverly argues, is only a prologue, a necessary but rather uninteresting preparation for what is to follow. The true climax will arrive once he assumes kingship. This smart but trite link between life and drama is countered by Prospero's 'revels' speech delivered after the dancers at the masque vanish, in which he draws a similar but much more profound comparison:

Our revels now are ended. These our actors,
As I foretold you, were all spirits and
Are melted into air, into thin air;
And – like the baseless fabric of this vision –
The cloud-capped towers, the gorgeous palaces,
The solemn temples, the great globe itself,
Yea, all which it inherit, shall dissolve,
And like this insubstantial pageant faded,
Leave not a rack behind. We are such stuff
As dreams are made on, and our little life
Is rounded with a sleep.

(4.1.148–58)

The analogy here is implicit and understated. The 'revels' that the audience (both Shakespeare's and Prospero's) has just witnessed become a metaphor for Prospero's achievements as a magus, Shakespeare's work in the theatre and for life itself. Unlike Antonio, Prospero visualizes the climax of the drama of life as a melting away rather than a crescendo. The moment is experienced with either sadness and disappointment, or resignation, or acceptance and calm (depending on how one reads the play and the figure of Prospero), but not with the triumph and exultation that Antonio promises Sebastian. Multiple references from across the play (air, clouds, dreams, sleep) are gathered together in this speech. The well-chosen and vivid images of 'cloud-capped towers', 'gorgeous palaces', 'solemn temples' and the 'great globe' (that obviously refers to Shakespeare's own theatre as well as to the world at large) is an acknowledgement of the seductive grandeur of the vision, but the awareness of the transience of things overwhelms, and the vision is dismissed as 'baseless' and 'insubstantial'. The last three lines are among the most beautiful written by Shakespeare. Profound as they are, the dramatist refuses to indulge in lofty abstractions, but turns to short, simple diction. We are merely the 'stuff' of dreams, and life is, quite simply, a 'little' thing. The lines culminate in the word 'sleep', which has occurred several times before in the play (Miranda has been put to sleep, Alonso and others are overcome with drowsiness) but which here stands, quite clearly, for death.

While we have considered the play's metrical pattern, its diction, imagery and use of figurative language as separate categories here, we recognize that none of these systems is distinct or independent of each other. The semiotician Yuri Lotman, writes that a literary text is multisystemic, that is, each of its formal elements constitutes a separate system within it, but in the words of Eagleton (commenting on Lotman), 'These systems exist in dynamic interaction with each other, an interaction which includes collisions and disparities between them.' So, a word contributes to the poem's phonetic system even as its denotative and connotative meanings make up the play's lexicon and it might, in certain cases, constitute a figure of speech of speech as well. Like the actors in a play, the different elements of language work separately in order to together bring the work to completion.

Literary devices apart, music constitutes one of the important 'special effects' in *The Tempest*. The references to music and the actual songs that are performed contribute in no small part to the air of enchantment and mystery that pervades the play. Caliban is moved to dream and to weep by the 'sounds and sweet airs' on the island and Ferdinand is puzzled and enchanted by the sounds of Ariel's song. 'Where should this music be?' the prince wonders, 'I' th' air, or th' earth? / It sounds no more, and sure it waits upon / Some god o' th' island' (1.2.388–90). Later, Ariel claims that his music casts a spell on its listeners and that it is so powerful and sensual that it can actually be smelt (4.1.178) by them.

Stage directions calling for music abound: *Ariel, invisible, playing and singing* (1.2), *Ariel plays the tune on a tabor and pipe* (3.2), '*Solemn and strange Music*' (3.3), '*a strange hollow and confused noise*' (4.1) and '*Solemn music*' (5.1). While there is plenty of music in many of Shakespeare's comedies, the indoors staging of *The Tempest* at the Blackfriars would have allowed for singers and instrumentalists, and consequently, more frequent and perhaps more complex compositions. In fact, the tunes for two of Ariel's songs, composed by Robert Johnson, a lutist at James I's court survive, and we can assume that the role of Ariel must have been performed by an actor who was also a fairly skilful singer.

Eighteenth-century critic Samuel Johnson writes that the songs in the play (and he refers to Ariel's songs in particular) 'however seasonable and efficacious, must be allowed to be of no supernatural dignity or elegance, they express nothing great, nor reveal anything above mortal discovery'. But while the lyrics of the songs may not be particularly profound or philosophical, they do evoke distinct and powerful feelings through simple but moving words. The Renaissance theory, based on Neoplatonic philosophy, was that man-made music

reflected the celestial 'harmony of the spheres', the music supposedly created by the movement of the stars and planets in
relation to each other. Besides, just like the stars, music too
was believed to have a very palpable influence on humans.
Because this is akin to the effect of poetry (Sidney, for example, writes of the 'planet-like music of poetry') the music in
the play is in many ways analogous to the language of the play
itself – it moves, enchants and directs thought and action.

For the most part, the songs in *The Tempest* evoke in their
listeners a sense of peace and harmony. They serve to offset
the 'tempestuous noise of thunder and lightning', the crying
out, cursing and general air of confusion with which the play
begins, and the intense anger and bitterness often expressed
in the subsequent action. The first song is the light and lovely
lyric sung by Ariel, 'Come unto these yellow sands,' (1.2.376).
Ferdinand's response perfectly illustrates the Neoplatonic idea
of the soothing and harmonizing power of music. He says:

> Sitting on a bank,
> Weeping again the King my father's wreck,
> This music crept by me upon the waters,
> Allaying both their fury and my passion
> With its sweet air.
>
> (1.2.390–94)

Not only does music comfort Ferdinand as he mourns for his
father, but it also eventually leads him towards Miranda and
moves him to a simple and fresh lyricism that we don't in fact
see often in this young man. 'This music' is alive and moving (it 'crept' upon the waters), tender and sweet, yet powerful. Ariel's song that follows these lines ('Full fathom five
thy father lies' (1.2.397–403)) is as exquisite and talks of the
inevitability and strange beauty of death and the transformation it wroughts.

However, as is so often the case in *The Tempest*, Ferdinand's
words and the song can be more complex in their effect than
obvious at first. Ariel's earlier lyric ('Come unto these yellow

sands' (1.2.376–82)), lovely as it is, is followed by a rather jarring burden ('Hark, hark! Bow-wow, / The watch dogs bark, bow-wow' (1.2.383–4)). Similarly, after the beauty of 'Full fathom five' we are subject to the chorus of spirits going 'Ding dong' (1.2.404), something of a let down after the poetry of the song. It is as if Shakespeare deliberately inserts reminders of discord and disruption (after all, it is these same 'bow-wowing' spirits who later hunt down Caliban and company) even amid instances of beauty and harmony. As David Lindley writes: 'We are caught, therefore, in a double response to this song.' Just as in the case of the dialogue discussed in Chapter 1, the music too often invites somewhat conflicting reactions from the reader.

Ariel's 'solemn music' lulls the entire shipwrecked party to sleep, except for Antonio and Sebastian who remain untouched by it. Not for the first time in Shakespearean drama, the villainous and dastardly characters are immune to the transforming powers of music (Caliban is a significant exception to this). Oddly enough, it is the enchanting music that gives the two men the opportunity they need to plot their conspiracy. Eventually, however, Ariel's song, brief, foreboding, even slightly reproving, is sung in Gonzalo's ear and stalls them.

There are a number of songs in the Stephano–Trinculo episodes, drunken and bawdy little numbers that Alden and Virginia Vaughan describe as 'entertaining but of scant importance to the plot'. While this is true, these ditties are interesting in that they are among the few songs unscripted and undirected by Prospero. These unruly rebels are among the few characters in the play who do not sing to Prospero's tune, though they eventually pay for it. Caliban is also punished for his freedom cry, which is accompanied by a song in which he imagines a life without forced labour:

No more dams I'll make for fish,
Nor fetch in firing at requiring,
Nor scrape trenchering, nor wash dish.
Ban' ban' Ca-caliban,

Has a new master, get a new man.
Freedom, high-day; high-day freedom, freedom high-
day, freedom.

(2.2.176–82)

Caliban's song is neither as poetic as some of his speeches are,
nor does it become reality, but the point of this particular
spontaneous melody is simply to show that he can hope and
sing, albeit in his master's language.

Ariel also has a couple of unprompted songs later in
the play. He promises, in song, to execute Prospero's commands 'Before you can say "come" and "go"' (4.1.44). Unlike
Caliban's song, this one delights in labour and makes light
of the spirit's servitude to Prospero. Ariel's last song is also a
spontaneous outburst. The famous 'Where the bee sucks, there
suck I' (5.1.88–94) is a lovely, semi-pastoral vision of freedom. Both these songs end with Prospero tenderly declaring
his affection for his 'dainty Ariel' (5.1.95). Clearly, Prospero
too is moved by music and is less insistent, as the play draws
its end, on directing all of it himself.

## Masque

One of the most unusual features of *The Tempest* is the inclu-
sion of a masque in the play. As outlined on page 10, the
Jacobean masque was a popular form of court entertainment and enhanced the pomp and circumstance of the royal
court, even as it called attention to the court as a place of
cultural accomplishment. A few critics have even claimed
that the entire play is a type of extended masque, though
the five-act structure and complex plot make this argument
rather difficult to sustain. Others have viewed the entire
masque within the play with some amount of derision and
even speculated that the masque is not by Shakespeare, but
was introduced sometime later in the play's history. However,
we should remember that masques were held in high esteem

in Shakespeare's time and the early indoor staging of *The Tempest* made it possible for him to incorporate such a show into the fourth act of the play.

The language of the masque is very poetic, but unlike the rest of the play, the poetry is elevated and formal as in lines like these:

> Hail, many-coloured messenger, that ne'er
> Dost disobey the wife of Jupiter;
> Who, with thy saffron wings, upon my flowers?
> Diffusest honey-drops, refreshing showers,
> And with each end of thy blue bow does crown
> My bosky acres and my unshrubbed down,
> Rich scarf to my proud earth.

> (4.1.76–82)

The masque is a spectacular mixture of this kind of stylized poetry, music, lavish costumes and dances that must have delighted most Renaissance theatregoers. It is staged to celebrate 'A contract of true love' (4.1.84) and to bestow blessings on the young couple, just as Shakespeare's play itself was staged to celebrate the betrothal of Princess Elizabeth. The three goddesses, the 'temperate nymphs' (4.1.132) and the 'sunburned sicklemen' or reapers (4.1.134) respectively represent the divine and the human, the feminine and the masculine elements, which together are fundamental to the natural order. The goddesses are carefully chosen – Iris, the messenger goddess, whose symbol is the rainbow, Ceres, the goddess of agriculture and Juno, the queen of the gods and the goddess of light, represent the union of air, earth and fire. The entire cosmos blesses the young couple in unison.

Ceres, the 'most bounteous lady' (4.1.60), the goddess of the earth and harvest, is essential to the masque, as she stands for fecundity and the rejuvenation of life, both of which need to be invoked at a betrothal. The landscape invoked by the masque is clearly symbolic. It is rich, fertile and bursting with renewed life. Ceres inhabits a world of 'rich leas', covered with 'wheat, rye, barley, vetches, oats and peas;' and 'turfy mountains' filled with 'live nibbling sheep' (4.1.60–3). This description of the land is very different from the savage and surreal landscape of the island that Caliban so loves, and also from the abstracted utopia that Gonzalo dreams of. In contrast, the landscape of the masque is shaped by husbandry. In fact, the thatched barns, the riverbanks and 'spongy April' (4.1.65) evoke a European landscape that is as temperate, comforting and familiar to the play's audience as it is beautiful. This is the world to which Ferdinand and Miranda truly belong, to which they will return and where they will bear children and prosper.

The language of landscape in the masque is also iconic in that it evokes the moral landscape of the play. The relationship being celebrated here will be happy, but marked by goodness and moderation. After all, the masque was preceded by Prospero repeating to his future son-in-law the dire consequences of permitting 'th' fire i' th' blood' (4.1.53) to rule and even contemplating sexual relations before marriage, and the actual masque itself has a very specific rhetorical function (as far as Ferdinand is concerned) – it is to drive home the lesson of chastity. It is significant that the gods of love and sexual desire, Venus and Cupid, are kept away by the other deities of the masque. Pagan goddesses and images of fertility and growth notwithstanding, the masque celebrates controlled sexual desire 'Till Hymen's torch be lighted' (4.1.97). This is in contrast to Caliban's savagery that manifests itself in unruly and violent lust. Prospero seems to see the masque as a way of communicating to the young people, through the harmony and structure of the entertainment itself, the harmonies underlying the universe, and the value and beauty of happiness and desire experienced within structures and boundaries.

The masque also gives the reader occasion to ponder both political power and the power of theatre. The opulent Jacobean masque also had a very clear purpose: it was a display of royal power even as it served to further that same power. Prospero seems aware that he must perform before 'the rabble' (4.1.37) and show them, including Ferdinand, that he can call up spirits at will 'to enact / My present fancies' (4.1.121–2). At the same time, however, Prospero's references to his 'fancies' and to the 'vanity of mine art' (4.1.41) are self-deprecatory even as they are arrogant. He seems to be aware of the fragile foundations of power, that it is not built on anything more substantial than mere display, perhaps. There is also a sense that theatre itself is a somewhat frivolous, self-indulgent pastime. He needs to keep the 'rabble' enthralled as 'they expect it from me' (4.1.42). However, in spite of this ironic distance from the show he is about to direct, Prospero is also aware that it is significant and necessary.

The masque begins with the command: 'No tongue, all eyes. Be silent!' (4.1.59). The artist dominates and commands the viewer's senses. The viewer is captive to the workings of theatrical power and can do little else but watch. But at the same time, the same lines recognize that the audience's cooperation is necessary in order for the show to work and the audience can potentially disrupt the illusion being staged. Hence, Prospero needs to command or plead with Ferdinand to 'Hush and be mute, / Or else our spell is marred' (4.1.126–7). The artist is also subject to the audience's will.

But the audience, like the fictive audience in the play, is startled at the suddenness with which the staging ends. The reapers and nymphs barely begin their dance when '*Prospero suddenly starts and speaks; after which, to a strange hollow and confused noise, they heavily vanish*' (4.1). The vision of harmony and beauty ends on a note of bewilderment and chaos. Prospero is clearly extremely agitated and recalls 'that foul conspiracy / Of the beast Caliban and his confederates / Against my life' (4.1.139–41). How does one explain the movement from harmony to discord and what is the reason for Prospero's excessive perturbation? It certainly bewilders Ferdinand, and Miranda claims that she had never seen her father 'with anger so distempered!' (4.1.145). This movement from pleasure to frustration is a pattern that is repeated throughout the play: Caliban first loves Prospero and Stephano and then feels betrayed by them; Antonio and Sebastian almost succeed in their plans but are thwarted; Prospero regains his dukedom but must give up his art. It is this pervasive unease and disappointment that makes it difficult to characterize the play as comedy. Harmony is consistently disrupted and happiness diluted.

Like much else in the play, this textual moment also lends itself to multiple interpretations. Looked at from the perspective of the political power-play that *The Tempest* stages, the intrusion of Caliban into Prospero's consciousness even at a moment of celebration and joy possibly indicates Prospero's awareness of the fragility of his power and the fact that it can easily be toppled. It perhaps also signals doubt, albeit momentary, regarding the legitimacy of his claim to the island. If one prefers to read *The Tempest* as a play about making art, particularly theatre, this moment of disruption and distress might point to the difficulty of sustaining a literary or theatrical illusion when life and reality constantly intrude. The reminder of Caliban's 'foul conspiracy' also serves to reinforce that not all people are moved to morality and goodness and that art doesn't always reform. The traditional masque always ended in order, this was crucial to honour the benevolent and successful rule of the monarch. The grotesque and unruly 'antimasque' figures (Caliban can be read as one) appeared early on in the narrative but were always dismissed at the end. In Prospero's masque, however, Caliban is remembered at the end. But by inverting the traditional structure, Shakespeare makes us think about the meaning of political power: Is it really absolute or is it constantly threatened by foul conspiracies of kind or the other? He also makes us think about the scope and extent of the power enjoyed by an artist: How real and substantial is the power of creating illusions (one should remember that the famous revels speech discussed on page 94, in which Prospero ponders 'the baseless fabric of this vision', appears only a few lines after the masque's sudden closure)? The unexpected conclusion to the masque also reminds us of the disappointments and frustrations that lurk behind life's most joyous moments.

# Reading *The Tempest* 'intertextually'

It is important to recognize that any literary text is not an isolated work complete unto itself. It was composed and received in a complex sociocultural moment, which definitely impacted it, and it was also composed with an awareness of other works of literature that preceded it. It is therefore part of a network of mutual influences and exchanges. In *Shakespearean Negotiations*, Stephen Greenblatt describes textuality as 'a subtle, elusive set of exchanges, a network of trades and trade-offs, a jostling of competing representations'. In other words, all texts are a result of, and themselves participate in, a dynamic circulation of social and literary energy and influence. The term 'intertextuality' refers to the inevitable interconnectedness between texts. Every text alludes to, quotes, revises or is at least influenced by other texts that surround it. It is to return to Bakhtin's term, 'heteroglossic' or multivoiced, and writing is always necessarily rewriting, echoing and quoting. It is therefore part of a fabric of 'literary discourse', and when reading one particular text, other literary texts nearly always obtrude on our consciousness. *The Tempest* too is enriched by the imprints of other literary and non-literary texts.

While intertextuality is not simply about identifying sources and allusions but also about placing a text in the midst of a network of other texts that are similar as far as style or subject matter are concerned, it is useful to begin by pointing out allusions and possible sources for the play. Any good edition of *The Tempest* will provide the numerous literary allusions in the play. Just two of them – the goddesses in the masque who are obviously taken from Greek mythology and the last two lines of the epilogue ('As you from crimes would pardoned be / Let your indulgence set me free.' (Epilogue 19–20)) that is a reference to the Lord's Prayer – indicate the range of Shakespeare's influences. As far as a possible source for the play is concerned, while Shakespeare, like other authors of his time, did not hesitate to take his storylines from other literary works, *The Tempest* is unusual in that no single work can be identified as its source. It does have similarities with a very popular romance, *The Mirror of Knighthood*, that was translated from a Spanish story in 1580, which tells the story of a royal prince who studies magic and goes to live on an island with his infant children. It also slightly resembles a German text *Die schöne Sidea* in which a defeated king escapes to an island with his daughter and engages in magic. Though there are parallels between these tales and Shakespeare's play, the resemblances are slight, and neither of these texts can be called a distinct source. But they do tell us something about the interest in stories in the romance genre and as Alden and Virginia Vaughan write, they demonstrate 'Renaissance Europe's fascination with exotic tales of magicians, wizards, strange beasts, enchanted islands and romantic love – a broad intertextual framework that underlies Shakespeare's play'.

*The Tempest* also needs to be placed in the context of other literary texts that are not sources or even passing allusions, but which might more profoundly impact the way in which the play makes meaning. The two classical texts that the play has been read against are two pieces of ancient Latin literature that both Shakespeare and his audience would surely have been familiar with – Virgil's epic *Aeneid* and Ovid's *Metamorphoses*.

Like the *Aeneid*, *The Tempest* too begins with a storm, and like Virgil's hero, Prospero too is exiled from his homeland and takes the responsibility of securing his child's future very seriously. The *Aeneid* is also read as an imperial epic which tells the story of the founding of Rome. Besides, Ferdinand's exclamation on seeing Miranda ('Most sure the goddess / On whom these airs attend!' (1.2.422–23)) is an echo of Aeneas's line 'O *dea certe*' ('Oh, thou are surely a goddess!') when he encounters his mother Venus. When the court party talk of the princess Claribel's marriage to the King of Tunis, Gonzalo reminds them that Tunis was once Carthage, the city of Dido, the *Aeneid*'s tragic female figure. Given the fact that Dido's love affair with Aeneas ends in abandonment and sorrow, the allusion also hints at the courtiers' doubts about the success of Claribel's alliance. The Ferdinand–Miranda story is, however, a happy reworking of the Aeneas–Dido legend. Like Aeneas, Ferdinand does find his beloved after a shipwreck, but unlike the unhappy couple of the epic, the love story in the play ends on a note of joyful hope.

The other Latin text whose presence in *The Tempest* is discernable is *Metamorphoses*, a favourite of many Renaissance writers. Prospero's 'Ye elves of hills' speech is a rough paraphrase of the witch Medea's song in Ovid's poem as translated into English by Arthur Golding in the sixteenth century:

> Ye charmes and Witchcrafts, and thou Earth, which both with herbe and weed
> Of mightie workings furnishes the Wizardes at their need;
> Ye airs and winds: ye Elves, of Hilles, of Brookes, of woods alone,
> Of standing Lakes, and of the night, approach ye every one
> Through helpe of whom (the crooked banks much wond'ring at the thing)
> I have compelled streams to run clean backward to their spring.
> By charms I make the calm seas rough, and make the rough seas plain,
> And cover all the sky with clouds and chase them thence again.
> By charms I raise and lay the winds, and burst the viper's jaw,
> And from the bowels of the earth both stones and trees do draw,
> Whole woods and forests I remove; to make the mountains shake,
> And even the earth itself to groan and fearfully to quake.
> I call up dead men from their graves; . . .

Shakespeare improvises the first few lines, adding detail and appealing imagery (as discussed on page 45) and then turns to Ovid's text to provide the details that will illustrate the power of magic. In contrast to the light and fanciful opening lines,

Prospero's reference to calling up storms, bedimming the sun and calling forth the dead from their graves is dark and disconcerting. The fact that Prospero is echoing the evil Medea, allies his magic with hers and renders it troubling and certainly most unchristian. Medea uses her magic to effect revenge, whether Prospero too does so in a similar fashion is up for debate. But then Prospero does renounce his magic at the end of these lines so distancing himself from the world of pagan and female forces, from both Medea and the female witch of the play, Sycorax, who can also be associated with Medea (Stephen Orgel has suggested that Sycorax's name is derived from one of the names for Medea 'Sythian raven' – 'korax' meaning raven). Apart from this single reference, Jonathan Bate argues that the influence of Ovid is pervasive through the play. The Latin poem deals with physical metamorphosis or transformation and the theme of change through ill-fortune, old age, death, love and encounters with the strange, with oneself and one's past – all of which are themes that are quite easily discernable in Shakespeare's play.

Apart from classical sources, we can hear echoes of other Renaissance writers in *The Tempest*. Gonzalo's speech outlining his vision of the ideal commonwealth on the island (2.1) borrows from Renaissance French courtier and philosopher Michel de Montaigne's 1580 essay 'Of the Cannibals'. In this piece, Montaigne argues that both 'civilization' and 'barbarism' are relative constructs. Of the people of Brazil, he writes that there is nothing he can see 'that is either barbarous or savage, unless men call that barbarism which is not common to them'. Indeed, he says, it is Europe which has deformed nature 'by our artificial devices' and the 'pleasure of our corrupted taste'. This, according to Montaigne, is truly savage. The Brazilian Indians have already created the perfect society that Europeans should aspire to, he writes in the lines appropriated by Shakespeare and given to Gonzalo:

> It is a nation; I would answer Plato, that hath no kind of traffic, no knowledge of letters, no intelligence

of numbers, no name of magistrate, nor of political superiority, no use of service, of riches or of poverty, no contracts, no successions, no partitions, no occupation but idle, no respect of kindred, but common, no apparel but natural, no manuring of lands, no use of wine, corn, or metal.

Montaigne's reflections on civilization and barbarism have clearly influenced *The Tempest*. The complex portrayal of Caliban and equally complex representation of the Europeans as both faithful and upright as well as corrupt and power hungry surely has something to do with Montaigne challenging the Renaissance tendency to link morality and civilization to ethnicity, race and religion.

There are also the two pieces of Renaissance travel writing mentioned earlier. Historian and traveller William Strachey, author of the letter 'True Repertory of the Wrack', was in a Virginia-bound ship in 1609 when a terrible storm landed him and his fellow voyagers in the Bermudas. The storm is graphically described by Strachey as a 'dreadful storm and hideous . . . swelling and roaring as it were by fits . . . at length did beat all light from heaven'. This evocative piece of writing must have kindled Shakespeare's imagination. The magical appearance of 'St. Elmo's Fire' is also described by Strachey as 'an apparition of a little round light, like a faint star, trembling and streaming along, with a sparkling blaze half the height of the main mast'. It shot about the ship frightening and fascinating the passengers, and becomes, in Shakespeare's play, Ariel who flames about Alonso's ship, terrifying the travellers. The islands (the Bermudas) that the shipwrecked sailors find themselves in are described by Strachey as 'dangerous and dreaded' islands that 'be called commonly the Devil's islands and are feared and avoided of all sea travellers alive above any other place in the world'. In almost the same breath, he describes the islands as 'habitable and commodious as most countries of the same clime and habitation'. As discussed on page 34, this paradoxical depiction of the land as both inviting and fearful is characteristic of Shakespeare's depiction of the enchanted island.

Strachey's fellow-traveller Sylvester Jourdain also wrote of the hurricane and the landing in the Bermudas in his travelogue 'Discovery of the Bermudas'. He also describes the island in equally conflicting ways. Moreover, Jourdain depicts the storm as both a physical and moral ordeal and turns to the language of providence and the will of God to explain the sufferings and eventual deliverance of the sailors. In *The Tempest* too, there is a sense of a higher power at work, which can save as well as punish, and Prospero would be its human representative.

Our reception and interpretation of *The Tempest* can be shaped by our awareness of other works that might not be directly or even implicitly alluded to in the play. Our understanding of Prospero's magic, for example, can be complicated if we have some knowledge of other Renaissance writings on magic: some of which condemn magic and see it as satanic and destructive and others (such as the Neoplatonic thinker Pico della Mirandola's famous humanist text *Oration on the Dignity of Man* that passionately argues that while God certainly made man, man is still the 'maker and moulder' of himself) which imply that all human knowledge is a legitimate way of attaining power and self-determination. Plays dealing with magic such as Robert Greene's *Friar Bacon and Friar Bungay* (ca. 1589) and Christopher Marlowe's *Dr. Faustus* (1592), both of which feature magicians who renounce their magic as evil, or who are both empowered and destroyed by its transformative power, constitute the 'discursive context' of *The Tempest*. Similarly, if one wishes to pay attention to the imperial/colonial theme one must place Shakespeare's play amid the hundreds of other Renaissance travel writings on travel, imperial ambition and racial and cultural difference. Some of these, we will find, glorify the colonial mission. For instance, geographer and compiler of a vast collection of contemporary travel writing Richard Hakluyt writes that the Virginia project will enhance the glory of God, Queen and country, apart from bringing in vast revenue. Others, most well known of whom is the Spanish missionary Bartolme de Las Casas, are appalled at the brutal treatment of the natives of the Americas and wonders if the hunger for power and wealth that provoked Europeans to settle these lands have unfortunately resulted in Christians forgetting Christian virtue and mercy.

Reading *The Tempest* intertextually will then involve alerting ourselves to these and other texts. Some of these, such as Montaigne and Ovid, assert themselves and call our attention, others are more shadowy subtexts, but together they render our response to the play more sophisticated. We reach a better understanding of how the language of *The Tempest* works when we realize that it is part of a rich and varied literary fabric, which it echoes, alludes to, revises and speaks to in one way or the other. Oddly enough, our response to the play can be shaped even by texts that were written centuries *after* Shakespeare's play, as we will see in the next chapter.

# Writing matters

This chapter has focused largely on the deliberate and self-conscious use of literary language in the play. Identifying and accurately describing figures of speech and other instances of literary language is a crucial part of close reading. When writing about the play, one has to demonstrate how the formal aspects of the play (its structure, its stylistic devices) shape our own responses and direct or divert our sympathy from characters and situations. Even as you attempt a study of the play's formal properties, you must also be able to move these observations towards an examination of its thematic concerns. This section includes questions that will provide you the opportunity to further explore literary form and language. You could attempt to respond to these questions in short essays of one–two pages.

## *Structure and sound*

We have discussed some of the effects of the play's classical structure and its observation of the unities of time, place and action. The unity of place draws attention to links between place, identity and politics, and the fact that the action is packed within a 24-hour period leaves plenty that is unsaid and also complicates our understanding of beginnings, endings and resolutions. Use these questions to continue thinking about the impact of the structure of the play.

**1** According to the 'pyramidal plot structure', every play's plot structure should have the following components: (i) exposition, (ii) rising action, (iii) climax, (iv) falling action, and (v) resolution. Shakespeare chooses to begin *The Tempest* with the storm and has Prospero recount the earlier story of Antonio's treachery and all that followed. Consider, (i) whether the storm is an effective opening to the play and (ii) if the technique of Prospero's exposition in Act I is an elegant and effective way of providing background information. How do you think our attitude to Prospero and Antonio would have changed if the prehistory had actually been part of the play?

**2** Does the play have a climax? Prospero's renunciation of magic can be identified as a possible climax, Alonso and party's meeting with Prospero can also be the climax, as can Prospero's revelation to Alonso that Ferdinand is alive and well. Similarly, Caliban's defeat can also be considered the climax. Which of these strikes you as the most climactic moment in the play? Or, is there any other moment you'd identify as the climax? Think about how your understanding of the play's central theme shifts depending on where you locate the climax of the play.

**3**  What do you look for in a satisfactory resolution to a story? Identify the features of the play's ending that give the plot a conventional resolution. To what extent is the conclusion unsatisfactory and even incomplete?

**4**  While conflict is central to fictional narrative, especially drama, it can be argued that *The Tempest* does not really have conflict since we know that Prospero is managing the course of events right from the start. Do you agree with this? Discuss.

**5**  *The Tempest* is a beautiful piece of writing. The blank verse, alliteration and other sound effects (along with the other aspects of style and structure we've discussed in this chapter) contribute to this. However, it could also be argued that the story itself revolves around fairly unattractive aspects of human experience: resentment, revenge, slavery and power. Does the play's poetry and its aesthetic dimension in general make us more aware of the injustices and darkness of life, or do you think it serves to mask them so that we are swept away by the poetry and, as a result, overlook the toughness and cruelty? Discuss.

## *Diction*

**1**  We have traced two of the words ('delicate' and 'strange') that recur through the play. Track other such words (vocabulary connected to freedom and bondage, for example, or words denoting memory and recollection, or those connected to transformation and change of one kind or another). How do these lexical patterns connect to and tell the story?

**2**  Investigate the origins of the word 'tempest'. Look at the word in other contexts. In what way does a greater

knowledge of the word deepen your understanding of
the play/themes/characters?

**3**  We have discussed different kinds of rhetoric (curses,
prayers, humour) in the play. Another very distinct
and easily identifiable kind of language that is
characteristic of comedy is the language of romantic
love. Shakespeare not only enjoys experimenting with
the language of romance in his work, but he also likes
to explore the relationship between language and love.
Can language be an adequate vehicle to represent love?
Do we fall in love because a certain kind of romantic
discourse pleases and excites us? Is the object of desire
constructed rhetorically in such a way that we are
often in love with the idea or image of a person rather
than a 'real' person? These are questions he explores in
many of his plays. Ferdinand is the obvious romantic
lover of *The Tempest*. Examine Ferdinand's language
in Acts 1.2 (when he first sees Miranda), 3.1 (as he
labours over the logs and is alone with her for the first
time) and 4.1 (when Prospero gives him permission to
marry his daughter).

**a**  Do you think Ferdinand's romantic language is
fresh and original?

**b**  How does Miranda, unschooled in the ways of
courtly love, respond to him? Is her language
different from his?

**c**  Contrast Ferdinand's language to that of Caliban.
How does each of the two young men talk about
sexual desire? What is each one's attitude to forced
labour?

**d**  Does Shakespeare succeed in giving Ferdinand a
distinct and interesting personality? Or does he
remain a flat character, even as he is crucial to the
romantic plot?

   **e**  Does anyone else talk of love (not necessarily in the romantic sense) in the play? If so, who? And how does the playwright use language to convey the subtleties of non-romantic love?

**4**  Do you agree that the characters in the play have distinct styles of speech? Select any two characters and compare key speeches to elaborate on your response.

**5**  Closely study the language that Prospero uses to degrade Caliban and also the language that Miranda uses towards Caliban. Explain your observations and conclusions.

## *Figures of speech and symbols*

**1**  Literary language is often symbolic, that is, concrete objects serve to suggest other ideas and states of being. In fact, one of the defining characteristics of literary language is that one is provoked to the sensuous appreciation of the concrete object (the storm, the monster, the split oak, for example), even as one is invited to ponder what else these objects could stand for. As Coleridge writes, the excellence of art consists in 'a union and interpretation of the universal and particular'. This aesthetic, what has been termed the 'concrete universal', was especially emphasized in nineteenth-century criticism. While it is important to refrain from seeing every concrete entity in a story as symbolic, that is, standing for something else that is abstract and universally recognizable, there might be a few symbolic elements in the play. Discuss how some of these elements in the narrative might function as symbols signifying other things, even as they are interesting and significant in their own right:

   **a**  the storm

   **b**  the island

c   the cloven pine that Ariel is imprisoned in and
released from

d   Prospero's staff and robe

e   Prospero's cave and Caliban's rock

2   Metaphors make meaning through association and
comparison. Consider the plummet metaphor that
occurs twice in the play. In 3.3, Alonso declares that
he'll seek his son 'deeper than e'er plummet sounded'
(3.3.101). Prospero later says he'll 'drown his book'
'deeper than did ever plummet sound' (5.1.56).
Find out what a plummet is, and think about how
Shakespeare uses it to convey meaning. Also, discuss
whether the mechanical tenor (the plummet is a kind
of mechanical device) takes away from the poetry of
the lines. Do you think it is a coincidence that the two
men of authority in the play (Alonso and Prospero) use
a very similar metaphor?

3   We have considered how the sea is personified in the
play. Some of the grandeur and power of these lines
by Alonso also come from the personification of the
sea:

> Methought the billows spoke and told me of it;
> The winds did sing it to me, and the thunder –
> That deep and dreadful organpipe – pronounced
> The name of Prosper.
>
> (3.3.96–9)

Consider how the speaking sea and singing winds in
these lines add to the terror felt by Alonso. How do we
respond to Alonso, who has done his share of wrong
in the past, as he utters these lines?

4   The sea certainly dominates the play, but the land
is also evoked metaphorically. In 2.1, the island is
described as an apple and is compared to a wench, it
has rotten lungs in 1.2 and is likened to a maze in 3.3.

Locate these figures of speech and discuss how they convey the characters' response to the island.

**5**  Sleeping and dreaming are both real events in the plot and evoked as tropes: Miranda falls asleep for part of Act 1, most of the court party too sleep in 2.1, Prospero says life is 'rounded with a sleep' (4.1.158), Caliban cries 'to dream again' (3.2.143) while Gonzalo dreams of his utopia. There are several other references as well. What does the language of dreaming and sleeping convey about characters' psychological and spiritual states and needs? Pick out references to dreaming and sleeping in the play and discuss their significance.

## Masque and music

**1**  In your view, does music play an important role in the play or is it merely entertaining?

**2**  Do you think the masque is important to the action or, like the music, is it merely an entertaining interruption?

## Intertextuality

**1**  The chapter you have just read pointed out some of the important allusions in the play. Select one or two of them, do further research on them and read up the original texts or stories being referred to. Follow this up with a brief discussion of how the allusions add to the depth of meaning and how knowledge of it alters your response to the play?

**2**  Shakespeare certainly had other texts in mind or was motivated by them as he wrote his play. Does the play suggest to or remind *you* of other texts, maybe more contemporary ones, that you have encountered? How does the evocation of these other texts impact the way you respond to *The Tempest*? In other words, how do you read the play as an intertextual document?

3 Compare and contrast the relationship of either Prospero and Miranda, Prospero and Caliban, Prospero and Ariel and Prospero and Ferdinand with a similar relationship from another play, novel, film or television show.

# CHAPTER THREE

# Language through time

Shakespeare's contemporary and fellow-dramatist Ben Jonson's complimentary statement that Shakespeare is 'not of an age, but for all time' is well known. But both Jonson and Shakespeare would probably be astounded if they could witness the extent to which Shakespeare's work has become the property of a variety of peoples and cultures over the last four centuries. *The Tempest* is among the most highly regarded of the plays. It is taught in classrooms across the world, is a constant subject of academic criticism, and is repeatedly performed on stage and film. This play alone stands as testament to the enduring value of Shakespeare's writing.

Literature is an instance of language functioning as public discourse. There is no immediate personal relation between the writer and listener or reader, and the text can be read or performed later in time and place in contexts that writer could not have anticipated. So, *The Tempest* has been re-read and re-enacted and has spoken very differently to different generations and cultures. Whatever Shakespeare's original intentions, they are irrecoverably lost to us and, in any case, like all art, any control the writer had over his work was exercised only in the original moment of composition. Once the play was completed and made public, it became the property of readers and viewers. Both critical interpretations and stage and film performances have changed so much over the years that it sometimes seems like readers, directors and actors have encountered different plays. As Stephen Orgel writes: '*The*

*Tempest* is a text that looks different in different contexts, and it has been used to support radically differing claims about Shakespeare's allegiances.' This would seem to attest to the view of reader-response criticism that meaning resides in the reader rather than in the text and interpretations are dictated by the dominant interests and concerns of the social and political moment in which the text is approached rather than inherent in the text itself. But surely, the multiplicity of meaning that has been imposed on *The Tempest* does not come entirely from outside the play. The density of the language, its inherent ambiguity and dialogism, as explored in Chapter 1, have clearly encouraged an array of interpretations. As even reader-response critics such as Wolfgang Iser concede, 'The literary work cannot be completely identical with the text, or with the realization of the text, but, in fact, must be half way between the two.'

Besides, no single play by Shakespeare has inspired future writers of fiction, poetry and drama to the extent *The Tempest* has. These literary successors of Shakespeare have been moved to rewrite and revise the play, and the history of the 'appropriation' of *The Tempest* also demonstrates the ways in which the language of the play has been received through time. In what follows, we will trace the play's critical and performance history, as well as survey its rewritings.

## Critical commentary on *The Tempest*

The long and dynamic critical history of *The Tempest* raises several questions about the enterprise of criticism itself. What dictates critical readings? Are interpretations of a text essentially arbitrary even as individual critics seem absolutely certain of the correctness of their interpretation and project their own commentary as essentially the last word on the play? Or, does the literary text limit interpretations in some way? Literary criticism involves the work being studied, the context in which it was written and/or performed and the context in which it is read, as well as theories or assumptions we all have about writing, reading and criticism. The combination of these factors shapes critical commentary, and in the case of *The Tempest*, the combination has produced seemingly endless interpretations.

The poet John Dryden who co-wrote an early adaptation of the play in 1667 was among the first to produce written commentary on the play. Like many critics who came after him, he focused on Caliban. For Dryden, Caliban is sufficient proof of Shakespeare's fertile imagination and copious powers of invention. In Caliban, Shakespeare 'created a person which was not in Nature, a boldness which to first sight would appear intolerable: for he makes a Species of himself'. Whether there were real-life counterparts to Caliban was besides the point for Dryden, what matters is that he is invested by Shakespeare with a personality and style of speech that are credible within the context of the play. Dryden's commentary shaped other early criticism. Writing in 1712, the essayist Joseph Addison said that Caliban was the greatest of Shakespeare's creations because unlike most of the characters who populate his plays who were drawn from history or real life, Caliban 'was supplied out of his own Imagination'. Much criticism in the eighteenth century came from other authors like Addison, or from editors who were putting together critical editions of the play. In this century, Shakespeare was gradually becoming monumentalized and critics often turned their energies to proving his genius and authority. He was seen as combing the lyrical and dramatic, aesthetic and moral in ways unequalled by any English writer.

Nineteenth-century criticism nicely illustrates how interpretations of *The Tempest* emerge from the sociopolitical and cultural climate responding to the play's language in specific ways. The nineteenth century saw the rise of the English Romantic tradition, a tradition that produced its own master poets, and which was based on the belief in the ruling power of the imagination, which was seen by the Romantics as the source of human experience, morality and action. Shakespeare, whose reputation as *the* English poet was already well established, was the figure who poets of the nineteenth century turned to as they wrote about the poetic imagination and he was the writer against whom these later artists measured themselves. *The Tempest*, enchanting and magical as it is, was especially appealing to these nineteenth-century Romantic poet-critics. The poet Samuel Taylor Coleridge's comments on the play are particularly well known. Unlike prior criticism, Coleridge felt it important to identify the genre of the play. For Coleridge, the play is a romance, a recognizable and worthy literary category that does not aspire to be realistic and attests to the human ability to create fantastic and original worlds. Besides, writes Coleridge, the play appeals primarily to the *reader*'s imagination as well. It is because of this that he felt that stage productions that attempt to realize the vision of the play will always fall short, that the best and most genuine responses to the play 'ought to come from within, – from the moved and sympathetic imagination'. Coleridge is also among the first critics to note that Shakespeare's political opinions, whatever they might have been, are not easily discernable in the play; instead, he gives equal space to multiple points of view. Nor does Shakespeare play the moralist in any narrow sense; he celebrates humanity rather than reprimands it. Finally, Coleridge explicitly links all these effects to the language of the play. The Romantics were invested in a poetic language that was original and fresh even as it was the language of common speech. The language of *The Tempest* is admirable for Coleridge because it 'was not drawn from any set fashion . . . and is therefore for all ages'.

If Coleridge's commentary comes out of and is shaped by the Romantic Movement in English literature, other nineteenth-century criticism was also influenced by the intellectual and political climate of the day. Charles Darwin's book *The Origin of the Species* was published in the year 1859 and literary criticism was, perhaps inevitably, shaped by the ideas put forward in this momentous work. Darwin suggested that there was an animal, now extinct, that existed between man and his last ape ancestor. Consequently, Caliban began to be read as standing for this so-called missing link. Daniel Wilson's *Caliban: The Missing Link*, published in 1873 put forward this thesis. Wilson argued that Caliban was no monster or fish-like animal (a common assumption at the time) but 'essentially human', ' a novel anthropoid of a high type such as on the hypothesis must have existed intermediately between the ape and the man – in whom some spark of rational intelligence has been kindled'. The Caliban-anthropoid was part of the natural landscape of the island, and even the attempted rape of Miranda was not necessarily a morally evil act but simply the impulse of an animal. However, the 'spark of rational intelligence in him' made Caliban human enough to win our sympathies. Prospero's treatment of Caliban is linked to the ill-treatment of a hapless animal, even worse because that animal is something like a human. Caliban is also held up to be less villainous to the humans in the play, a notion based on Darwin's point that humans have greater intelligence and this makes them capable not only of greater goodness than any animal, but also of more evil. This reading inspired by Darwinian evolutionary theory challenged the more sentimental readings of the past that saw Prospero as the moral ground of the play.

As Britain established itself as the foremost imperial power in the world by the middle of the nineteenth century, *The Tempest* was soon recognized as a play that deals with colonial relationships. If the British Empire was a symbol of the nation's political might, Shakespeare was indicative of its cultural superiority, and critics were keen on finding connections between the two. *The Tempest* was thus seen as not only illustrating, but also as supportive of the colonial enterprise. While Caliban stayed resentful and ungrateful for the lessons of civilization imparted to him, it was still necessary for the intelligent and cultured races of the world to educate and humanize the less civilized. The play thus had valuable lessons for the English colonial labouring abroad. Besides colonialism, there were a number of other nineteenth-century readings that insisted that *The Tempest* illustrated ideas rang-ing from atheism to the dangers of democratic and political rebellion. In short, critics looked to the play to illustrate and complicate ideas and philosophies they themselves were pre-occupied with.

In the twentieth century, most commentary on the play took on the form of academic criticism, that is, it came out of universities and was written by professional full-time literary scholars. This not only led to a profusion of criticism, but it also meant that critics' theories about the meaning and func-tion of literary texts and their approach or methodology were deliberately considered and explicitly outlined. Every critical reading of a literary text is informed by a 'critical approach', a set of theories regarding how one reads, what one looks for in a text and how meaning is constructed. Several of these approaches have been applied to *The Tempest*. The section that follows is by no means a survey of critical approaches to literature. Instead, we will very briefly consider some of the perspectives that have dominated the study of *The Tempest*.

For several decades of the twentieth century, *'formalist' approaches* stood out. Formalist critics quite simply empha-size the 'form' of a literary work and see it as an object unto itself, that is, as unrelated to extrinsic issues like the histori-cal circumstances in which it was written or read. However, 'pure' formalist criticism is difficult to do well and quite rare, and formalist critics find themselves considering thematic issues, though always in relation to literary form. Formalist critics of *The Tempest* have focused on the interconnected metaphors and other figures of speech, the classical structure of the play, and how these contribute to the romance theme of harmony and unity. Spiritual and communal harmonies are connected to the harmony evident in the composition of the play itself. Formalists also insist that the only context really worth paying attention to in the criticism of a literary work is *other* literary works. Consequently, there have been a number of formalist essays on *The Tempest* that consider it in light of other plays by Shakespeare or in terms of its genre. The play has been read as the playwright's engagement with the conflict discernable in his tragedies between goodness and beauty on the one hand, and evil and malevolence on the other. In *The Tempest*, however, the beautiful and the good triumph. There is a shipwreck, but the passengers are saved and will go home. Similarly, hostility and revenge are transformed to harmony and reconciliation. The romance is thus a genre that not only reverses tragedy but also completes it. The critical assumptions behind these studies is that Shakespeare's plays are a single, unified body of work and individual texts are best studied in relation to the whole. *The Tempest* would thus be the culmination of all the other plays.

Frank Kermode, editor of the second Arden edition of *The Tempest* (1954) wrote a well-known introduction, which is also, broadly speaking, in the formalist tradition. Responding to those critics who insisted that *The Tempest* is a religious or political allegory, or that it tells us something about the life or personality of Shakespeare, Kermode attempted to convince readers that the play is best understood in terms of its genre. *The Tempest*, he says, is a kind of pastoral drama, and like pastoral poetry, it is concerned with the opposition between 'Nature' and 'Art'. However, while the traditional pastoral contrasts the purity and goodness of the natural world to the decadence of civilization, and celebrates the former, *The Tempest* makes a more complex point. While Caliban stands for the world of Nature and very often his bestiality comes off better than the corruption of Antonio, Stephano and Trinculo, who are representatives of civilization, unlike other commentators of his time, Shakespeare does not engage in a simplistic celebration of the natural and primitive. Caliban stands for nature without the benefit of education and is therefore crude, lustful, and incapable of goodness and humanity. 'Caliban is the ground of the play. His function is to illuminate by contrast the world of art, nurture, civility', writes Kermode. The true representative of Art in the play is Prospero. He is scholarly and educated and his knowledge, that is, magic, serves to make him virtuous and self-disciplined. It also gives him the powers necessary to control nature and to ultimately restore harmony at the personal and political levels. He therefore stands for Art at its best. Kermode's essay is extremely well known and is interesting in its methodology because even as it is concerned with the style and structure of the play itself (in the tradition of formalism), it also places *The Tempest* in the context of a network of other texts, including Montaigne, the Bermuda pamphlets and several writings all of which are concerned with the Nature versus Art contrast Kermode sees as central to the play.

*The Tempest* has also interested scholars who take the '*historicist approach*' to the study of literature. Historicists study a text in terms of its historical context, and look at how a variety of social, cultural and political influences shape the work. The literary text in this case is considered a historical utterance and is best understood by locating it amid forces and other texts that are often non-literary. Besides, critics have also argued that the play merits a specifically political reading: the play is a history play in that it emerges from a complex historical moment that needs to be understood in order to understand it, and it also is a political play in that it is shaped by the struggles for power and influence that characterize any time period, including the Renaissance. This view of literature was proposed and popularized by critics (the best known of who is Raymond Williams) who described themselves as professing the approach of '*cultural materialism*'. A literary text is 'materialist' in that it is affected by very real and tangible socio-economic forces and also in that it performs a politically charged function. It not only reflects history and politics, but it can also intervene in and shape them through its cultural influence. For the reader, the text therefore becomes a natural and inevitable site of debate for various political issues such as class, gender and race, among other things.

A historicist and political critical approach informed by cultural materialism has dominated the study of *The Tempest* for some decades now and has substantially altered the kind of questions critics have asked about the play. Many of the political readings of the play have come from the post-colonial perspective. *Post-colonial literary criticism* is invested in examining literature in terms of the historical phenomenon of colonialism. It is interested in the relationship between literary texts and the political, moral and cultural issues surrounding the establishment and making of empires. England's position as the prime imperial power of the nineteenth century and Shakespeare' status as a national cultural icon have made Shakespearean texts an attractive object for post-colonial study. *The Tempest* is in fact the first play that drew the attention of post-colonial critics who have, broadly speaking, seen it as an allegory of colonialism. The island setting, Prospero's settlement of it, along with his ill-treatment of Caliban has made him the prototype of the colonizer, while Caliban is seen as a representation of the colonized who is unjustly dismissed as wild, evil and savage, but who still has the ability and need to protest the wrong done to him, as Caliban does when he claims the island as his.

While there have been a number of post-colonial readings of the play in the last two decades or so, it should be remembered that the tendency to see the play as an allegory for colonialism is not a new one. As discussed above, *pro*-imperial readings dominated in the nineteenth century when English imperial power was at its zenith, Prospero was read as the dutiful colonizer and Caliban as the thankless native. A version of this reading emerged as late as 1947, when Wilson Knight commented on Caliban as the savage bestial creature and the play as an allegory for the British imperial effort 'to raise savage peoples from superstition and blood sacrifice . . . to a more enlightened existence'. However, *anticolonial* readings too existed before the arrival of post-colonial criticism as an established critical approach. Earlier critics too expressed sympathy for Caliban. Several commentators writing in the context of the abolitionist movements in the United States were sensitive to Caliban's thraldom. Even earlier commentary, whether sympathetic to Caliban or not, often associated him with Native Americans. In 1808, Edward Malone argued for the Bermuda pamphlets as among the possible sources for the play. The first critic to directly insist that Caliban was the portrayal of a Native American was Sidney Lee in 1898. He felt that Shakespeare learned about American natives from Renaissance travel accounts and also from those natives who were taken captive and exhibited in England. For Lee, Caliban is 'an imaginary portrait, conceived with matchless vigour and vividness, of the aboriginal savage of the new World' and *The Tempest* as a whole is 'a veritable document of Anglo-American history'. Several other English and American scholars joined Lee in arguing for *The Tempest* as Shakespeare's 'American play' and some went so far as to look for very specific locations in North America that matched the island. According to the Vaughans, whose book *Shakespeare's Caliban – A Cultural History* is a detailed study of the ways in which Caliban has been approached, interpreted and performed for the last four hundred years, this America-focused critical trend of the early twentieth century can be connected to the emerging cultural and political friendship between the United States and Britain after nearly a century of tension, and the consequent need to find the early shared history of the two nations inscribed in the work of Shakespeare. Even over half a century later, in 1972, Leslie Fiedler wrote that without doubt, 'America was in Shakespeare's mind' as he wrote *The Tempest* and that Caliban was a composite of natives from different parts of the Americas as well as the African slave. Fiedler argues, 'to say that Caliban was an Indian means that he was a problem, since the age had not been able to decide what in fact Indians were. And, in a certain sense, *The Tempest* must be understood as an attempt to answer that troubling question on the basis of both ancient preconceptions and new information about the inhabitants of the Americas'.

Terence Hawkes who is not a post-colonialist critic, but who focused on the plurality of meaning of the text and the difficulty of pinning it down to one final and determinate meaning also, however gestured towards post-colonialist readings when he noted that the play demonstrates how all cultures feel the need to divide the world into two basic categories, the 'human' and 'non human'. What's more interesting – and troubling – is 'when the division becomes blurred and uncertain'. This inability to make the distinction is what characterizes Trinculo's response to Caliban when he first sees him. Hawkes also makes an interesting connection between colonialism and writing drama. Like a colonist, the dramatist 'imposes the "shape" of his own culture, embodied in his own speech, on the new world, and makes that world recognizable, habitable, "natural," able to speak his language'. Conversely, the dramatist is also like the colonist. He too explores new areas of human experience, pushes the boundaries of culture, 'and makes the new territory over in his own image. He . . . opens up new worlds for the imagination'.

The overtly and self-consciously post-colonial readings of *The Tempest* were inspired by Hawkes's comments to some extent. The first of these was Stephen Greenblatt's essay 'Learning to Curse – Aspects of Linguistic Colonialism in the Sixteenth Century'. Greenblatt was the best known proponent of *New Historicist criticism*. New historicism like other 'historicist' criticism, believed that a literary work was best understood in terms of its sociocultural context. New historicists were different from traditional historicists in that they did not see context simply as background against which the literary work is read. They instead argued for a more dynamic relationship between text and context and said that literature was influenced by and in turn participated in and influenced historical reality. They also read literature as one among different kinds of discourses or narratives, all of which ought to be given equal attention. For example, while Montaigne and the Bermuda pamphlets constitute interesting backdrops to *The Tempest*, the play also needs to be read alongside them. These other documents, together with Shakespeare's play, have similar social and political effects, and, besides, it is of little account whether Shakespeare actually was conscious of these other texts or not. Consequently, Greenblatt places *The Tempest* alongside writings as varied as voyager's narratives to the Americas, papal bulls, Renaissance works on history and philosophy and Spanish oaths of allegiance. He concludes that the play is one among many narratives that engages with the peculiar dynamics of the encounter between a lettered and supposedly unlettered culture. Native Americans were paradoxically depicted by early modern Europeans as having no language at all and therefore as completely different from Europeans, *or* as being perfectly comprehendible, therefore, as exactly like the Europeans. The Europeans were unable to sustain the perception of both likeness and difference. Greenblatt discerns a similar dynamic operating in *The Tempest*.

This study opened the floodgates of post-colonial readings. While different scholars focus on various aspects of *The Tempest*, they all agree that the play cannot be relegated behind the high walls of the 'purely literary', that it has to be acknowledged as one among a number of texts that operate as colonial discourse, and that it not only reflects but also actually participates in its own way in the colonial enterprise. As Francis Barker and Peter Hulme put it, 'the ensemble of fictional and lived practices, which for convenience we will simply refer to here as "English colonialism," provides *The Tempest*'s discursive contexts'. Post-colonial criticism has disagreed with the critical tradition that idealizes Prospero as the good and benevolent magician. He is instead seen as the colonialist who wields different kinds of power. He has the power of magic, which he uses to cow down Caliban. (Peter Hulme sees the magic as analogues to the firearms with which the Europeans frightened and awed the Native Americans.) He also has the power of narrative – he takes on the role of official historian and all other versions of the past are dominated by his. He constantly tries to justify his takeover of the island: by equating Antonio's treachery with Caliban, by reminding Caliban of the rape attempt (though the attempt came after the takeover), by representing Caliban's growing resentment towards him as treachery rather than as the natural response to the usurpation of his land and by binding Ariel to him by reminding him of his servitude to Sycorax. Post-colonial criticism has demonstrated how, like all colonialist discourse, the play sets up a series of binary oppositions – Prospero versus Caliban, civilization versus savagery, good versus bad magic, beauty versus ugliness, Miranda versus Caliban and Ferdinand versus Caliban. As a result, Caliban is always set up as the 'other', the perpetual inferior and outsider, who colonialism needs to justify its own project. Post-colonial readings have also identified very specific parallels between the play and historical occurrences. For instance, Prospero's torment of Caliban has been equated to the torture of natives in America and the scene where Prospero sets dog-shaped spirits upon him is said to be drawn from the Spanish practice of using dogs to hunt down natives. While these post-colonial interpretations seem to focus on the political theme, they do not disregard the literary element. Readings are firmly based on the language and structure of the play. For instance, the masque has been seen as symbolic of the drama of power that the play enacts because Prospero's energies in both the masque and the larger play are directed towards the establishment of his power, and the Trinculo–Stephano subplot's relationship to the main plot has been explained by interpreting it as Prospero deliberately setting up a crude and overtly exploitative version of colonialism (Trinculo wants to abduct Caliban to England and exhibit him for money) against which his own, brutal as it is, comes off as better. Similarly, for Paul Brown, the pleasurable narrative, the strict observance of the unities of time, place and action, the music and general air of fantasy and harmony all together serve to cover up and mystify the brutal workings of power.

Post-colonial critics differ in their opinion on how successful the play is as colonialist discourse. While some argue that the play is more or less a straightforward representation of colonial discourse and that Prospero's power is all encompassing and ultimate, others point out that the play, and indeed all colonialist discourse, is ambivalent and contradictory. Prospero's power is far from absolute, a fact he is aware of. Threats of challenge and subversion are there right from the beginning (when the boatswain dismisses the aristocrats as troublesome and incompetent) and emerge over and over again. Caliban too can, after all, talk back. Anxieties regarding the nature and extent of colonial power therefore barely simmer below the surface of the play. Prospero's excessive anger at the disruption of the masque by his recollection of the 'foul conspiracy' of Caliban is also interpreted as a moment when a barely articulated anxiety regarding the legitimacy of his takeover of the island interrupts the vision of beauty, harmony and goodness that he, Prospero, has worked so hard to build. And although Caliban's conspiracy is quelled at the end, this anxiety remains. Greenblatt also reads the famous 'this thing of darkness I / Acknowledge mine' (5.1.275–6) as signalling not just ownership and control over the native, but also a moment of identification with him, 'some deeper recognition of affinity, some half-conscious acknowledgement of guilt'. Callaghan's reading (see page 63) of Prospero's obsessive recollection of Sycorax, whom he claims never to have met, serves to further complicate what this line tells us about Prospero's relations with Caliban. It could well connote 'an admission of paternity'. Callaghan is not simply asserting that Caliban is Prospero's son (there's obviously no way of telling for certain), her point is that Shakespeare's plot 'is deliberately vague and thus deliberately inclusive' about the sexual and the master–servant relations on the island. The scenario where masters often fathered their slaves, Callaghan points out was, after all, one of the hallmarks of colonial practice.

While earlier post-colonial criticism has tended to read the play as engaging with the European colonization of the Americas, later critics have included other parts of the world in their study. Paul Brown points out that the geography of British imperialism extended from the 'core' (Wales, for example), to the 'semi-periphery' (notably Ireland) and to the 'periphery' (America) and looks for connection and similarities between colonialist discourse operating at all three levels. Dympna Callaghan's essay discussed above argues that 'Ireland . . . might be understood as the sublimated context for

colonial relations in *The Tempest*, whose presence can be figured in the dense print of memory'. She reads Ariel as the more
cultured, lettered Irish and Caliban as the so-called Irish rabble, and traces parallels between the play and British attitudes
to Irish clothing, language, music and land. While Barbara
Fuchs does not discredit New World readings and even argues
for their importance, she conflates and collapses multiple locations and pays attention to the play's Mediterranean location.
For Fuchs, this is not just the classical world of the *Aeneid* and
*Odyssey*, but also a world dominated by the North African
Muslim powers who the English not only occasionally fought
with, but who were also trading and political partners. The
growing fear of Islam makes its way into *The Tempest*, and
the Muslim world is figured both in the fearful Sycorax who
is after all from Algiers on the Barbary Coast of North Africa
and in the Moorish king who the princess Claribel has been
forced to marry. The political necessity of the marriage as
well the horror with which it is viewed captures the contradictions in English engagements with the Muslim Mediterranean
world. Jerry Brotton also argued that New World readings
tend to overlook the fact that the island is located in the
Mediterranean (going by the fact that the shipwreck occurs as
the court party is returning from Tunis in North Africa). 'The
voyage undertaken by Alonso and his retinue from Naples to
Tunis in *The Tempest* was a voyage that traversed one of the
most contested stretches of water within the Mediterranean
world.' The play is less about colonialism, argues Brotton,
than an expression of English fears and insecurities accompa-
nying their forays into Mediterranean politics and trade.

Post-colonial studies in general and post-colonial criticism
of *The Tempest* in particular became widespread as the dis-
mantling of European empires saw vast numbers of people
dealing with and thinking about the impact of colonization on
their lives and nations, and many others too growing increasingly sensitive to the injustices that the political experience of
colonization had had on their fellow humans. Post-colonial
readings have not only had a profound impact on the ways in

which *The Tempest* has been taught and performed recently, but they have also transformed Shakespeare studies. Many more plays began to be read through the post-colonial lens and an entire subfield of 'post-colonial Shakespeare' was inaugurated. However, this manner of interpreting *The Tempest* has not escaped its share of criticism. It has been said that reading the play as post-colonial discourse offers no insight into the individual text and completely disregards the fact that the play is not just any other example of colonial discourse, but is primarily a literary artefact and this literariness surely impacts the way it makes meaning. It is also argued that there is no evidence that the seventeenth-century audiences saw Caliban as a native and indeed, there was no reason for them to do so: many details differentiate him from the travellers' reports of natives of the Americas. Besides, Sycorax is no native, she too is from the Old World, and is, like Prospero, a settler on the island. Further, in 1611, the situation was hardly 'colonial' in the strict sense and England could by no measure be described as a colonial power. These critics who have reservations about post-colonial readings also offer their own historicist readings of the play to counter the historicism of the post-colonial school. They examine the Virginia and Bermuda records and argue that if anything like 'colonial discourse' existed at all in those early years of New World travel and settlement, it was varied and complex. In fact, English writers spent more time attacking the Spanish and the idle and degenerate among their own party than in criticizing the natives. Besides, even if one acknowledges the colonial context as crucial to understanding the play, the play is hardly colonial discourse in the conventional sense. On the contrary, because it invites us to sympathize with Caliban, it is as anticolonial as it is colonial. Critic Meredith Skura offers an alternative reading of the play that has been influenced by Sigmund Freud's theory of human behaviour. Her *psychoanalytic reading* begins by critiquing post-colonial readings for offering no insight into the individual author and his individual psychology – in fact, all human experience in post-colonial readings is wrongly submerged into the political. Instead, Skura reads Caliban as standi for Prospero's (and all humans') other 'self', which in psyche analytic terms is primitive, infantile, greedy, orally oriented and megalomaniacal. It is only when Prospero is adrift from his familiar life in Milan does he meet his darker self, that is, Caliban. He also realizes that the brother, Antonio, who he had all along seen as part of his individual self, is really a distinct entity. The play is thus about a universal psychological experience – encountering and overcoming the infantile/ primitive self and coming into one's own as an individual.

Deborah Willis comments that post-colonial critics overlook the fact that Caliban is not really Prospero's antagonist, at least not seriously so. The real enemy is Antonio. The Prospero–Antonio conflict constitutes the central tension of the play, and it is in contrast to Antonio, rather than Caliban, that Prospero is celebrated. Shakespeare's Antonio comes out of a culture anxious about potentially rebellious aristocrats in general, and discontented younger brothers who were disadvantaged by the law of primogeniture in particular. The play is about all this, rather than colonialism, as it is also about how an individual's greed and aggression can override family and communal ties.

Though post-colonial readings have dominated the historicist study of *The Tempest*, there have been other historicist studies that have taken issue with the post-colonial perspective. David Kastan points out that the play is clearly set in the Mediterranean and the only references to the Americas in the play are to the Bermudas (referred to by Ariel as a distant fantastical space rather than the island itself), the god Setebos and Stephano and Trinculo's reference to Caliban as a 'dead Indian' (though Kastan argues that a careful reading of the scene would demonstrate that they don't mistake him for an Indian, they simply think he is a monster). Besides, Caliban is freckled and the son of a blue-eyed woman – surely, that's not the first image of a Native American or African slave that comes to one's mind? Kastan feels that post-colonial readings are motivated by the fact that we, critics and readers, occupy the post-colonial moment in history rather than anything in the play as such. Another kind of historicist reading based on the fact that the play was first enacted at a royal wedding is more enlightening. Expansion *is* a theme of the play, but it is expansion through securing political power through cooption of small states into larger ones (Alonso supports Antonio in order to get the vassalage of Milan) and through political marriages (Claribel with the unnamed Tunisian ruler, Miranda to Ferdinand). The play is, therefore, more about European dynastic concerns than it is about European colonization.

Post-colonial readings are not the only kind of political readings of *The Tempest*. The play has been read by critics interested in class and rank as an expression of tension between the wealthy aristocrats and the more humble born. This was an issue that comes up in the Virginia documents and it is visible in the play in the boatswain's impudence and in Trinculo's and Stephano's rebellion, which is, of course, eventually dismissed as grotesquely comic. The language of the play has also invited feminist critics to comment on it. *Feminist criticism* became popular in the late 1970s following the growing impact of political feminist movements in the Western world. Renaissance feminist critics have been invested in recovering the lost voices of women who lived during the time period, but, like other feminist critics, they have also been interested in the ways in which all language, including literary language, constructs and represents women and their experiences. Nineteenth-century works such as the 1832 *Shakespeare's Heroines* by Anna Jameson did consider the women in Shakespeare and commended Miranda for her 'modesty, grace and tenderness', but these older studies were, for the most part, not self-consciously feminist as such. Ania Loomba combines post-colonial and feminist readings in her study. She begins by exploring the role and influence of Shakespeare plays, including *The Tempest*, in Indian university education and moves on to a reading of the play. Caliban's masculinity is represented as fearsome and his sexuality as dangerous and excessive, recalling representations of the 'black rapist' in colonial and racist writing from different parts of the world. Prospero's language traps Caliban in this stereotype and he has no way of escaping it. Miranda is also a victim of the play's discourse, however. She becomes the passive white woman subject to her father's will. Her own needs and desires remain unarticulated. She is entirely schooled by Prospero to hate Caliban, to fall in love with Ferdinand, and her desires corroborates the will of her father. She is anxious to insist on her superiority to Caliban, but this only confirms her subordination to Prospero and the extent to which she has been brainwashed by him. The play also constructs that other woman Sycorax – demonic, sexually deviant and foreign – as the contrast to Miranda and further underscores Miranda's passivity. The fact that Miranda is the only living woman in the play indicates the absence of women from the colonial arena even as they play a role in it.

Ann Thomson too is of the opinion that while *The Tempest* might be an odd play for feminist critics to take up since there are such few women in it, perhaps that very feature makes it an interesting and provocative text. She considers Prospero's control of Miranda's sexuality before he hands her over to Ferdinand and the importance of her chastity, which is insisted on again and again in the play, both in the promises extracted from Ferdinand and in the masque that refuses to celebrate sexual desire outside of marriage. However, Miranda has to *also* stand for fertility and has the responsibility to bear heirs. In fact, *The Tempest* was the perfect play to perform at the wedding of Princess Elizabeth who, like Miranda, was beautiful, chaste, and, above all, obedient to a powerful father.

Other scholars such as Coppelia Kahn and Stephen Orgel have combined the feminist and psychoanalytic approaches and linked family structures, gender roles and sexual relations to the political relations in the play. Orgel points out that the play seems to erase mothers with Prospero's wife barely mentioned and Sycorax demonized. In fact, Prospero insists on taking on the maternal role as far as both Miranda and Ariel are concerned, and perhaps in a perverse and distorted way, towards Caliban as well. Miranda becomes the grounds for the quarrel between Prospero and Caliban. For Prospero, she is the symbol of his power, for Caliban, an instrument with which to people the isle with his offspring and establish his own rule. Soon after the nasty exchange between Prospero and Caliban in which they recall the rape attempt, Ferdinand appears and Miranda also serves as currency, the object that is exchanged between the men to create harmony between Prospero and his former enemies. However, other scholars have not found Miranda to be entirely passive. As we discussed on page 65, she also speaks out her own needs and desires and could, perhaps, be seen as more independent of Prospero than often given credit for.

The critical history of *The Tempest* is a long and interesting one. It demonstrates how the play speaks differently to readers over the years. The tension between formalist studies and historical studies, formalist approaches and political ones and even different kinds of historicist and political critical approaches continues, but the fact is that the best critical works, even those that cannot be described as formalist, pay attention to the play's formal and structural elements. The most impressive post-colonial, feminist and other readings are located in the language of the play. The fact that the language holds such immense and varied significance continues to make *The Tempest* provocative and exciting to critics.

## *The Tempest* on stage

*The Tempest* has also been staged in dynamic and ever-changing ways. Each era's performances have challenged earlier versions and have emerged out of changing ideas about theatre, the cultural significance of Shakespeare and the relationship between drama and society. *The Tempest* was, of course, originally conceived for the stage and as in the case of all play performances there are always a number of forces intervening between the play text and its viewership – the vision of the director, the imagination and talent of the actor and the material conditions of the theatre, for example. The fact that *The Tempest* has been realized so variously on stage is proof that there is nothing like an authentic or correct performance.

As is often the case with especially admired books turned into plays, television shows or films, there will always be those who feel that the performance can never live up to the worlds conjured in our head by the words on the page. Charles Lamb, nineteenth-century author and Shakespeare enthusiast, is one such disappointed viewer. He comments:

> But is *The Tempest* of Shakespeare at all a subject for stage representation? It is one thing to read an enchanter, and to believe the wondrous tale while we are reading it; but to have a conjurer brought before us in his conjuring-gown, with his spirits about him, which none but him and some hundreds of favoured spectators before the curtains are supposed to see, involves a quantity of the hateful incredible, that all our reverence for the author cannot hinder us from perceiving such gross attempts upon the senses to be in the highest degree childish and inefficient. Spirits and fairies cannot be represented, they cannot even be painted, – they can only be believed.

There are probably many other admirers of *The Tempest* who would agree with Lamb. *The Tempest* is for the 'inward eye' of the imagination. How can the magical world of the play and its moving poetry, even its complex politics, be produced on stage without falling short of the vision that exists in our minds? However, we should remember, that Shakespeare himself probably mainly thought of the play in terms of its enactment. The relatively short pieces of dialogue, the well-timed entrances and exits, the music and the costume changes (Ariel appears in four different costumes and the actor might have doubled as Ceres) all make for successful theatre.

We have already briefly touched on the first recorded performance of the play before James I in November 1611. The event was the betrothal of Princess Elizabeth; it was the season of Hallowmas or early winter. The persistent undertone of darkness in the play might have served as a sobering reminder of the season to come, while the joy and laughter that also asserts itself would have served as an antidote to winter. The indoor staging would have allowed the acting company to delight audiences with masque, music and sound effects from offstage. The marked contrast between the cosmic chaos of the storm and the social chaos of disobedient slaves and servants on the one hand, and the stately grandeur of the courtiers and their ladies seated in the candlelit hall and watching the tale unfold before them on the other, must have had some effect on that early audience's reception of the play. But we have no way of telling for certain.

It was not uncommon to rewrite Shakespeare plays during the Restoration, and in 1667, just 50-odd years after the first performance of *The Tempest*, writers John Dryden and William Davenant rewrote it as *The Tempest or The Enchanted Isle*. Dryden's Preface insists that the revision is a form of homage to Shakespeare and a way of ensuring that his work continued to live: 'So from old *Shakespear's* honour'd dust this day / Springs up and buds a new reviving play.' Dryden writes of the later authors as disciples of Shakespeare writing with 'the drops that fell from Shakespeare's Pen' while at the same time admitting that 'Shakespeare's Magick could not copy'd be / Within that Circle none walked butt he'. It could be said that Shakespeare's 'Magick' was certainly not successfully reproduced in the Dryden-Davenant play, though it is interesting as a unique piece of Restoration theatre. The authors simplified Shakespeare's language and put new emphasis on song and dance. They also gave Miranda a sister named Dorinda and made Sycorax Caliban's sister. Caliban's role was a relatively minor one (though he was probably played simply as a monster as that's how he is listed in Dryden–Davenant cast of characters) and Trinculo's role was expanded. What we get is a play with little poetry and a large dose of bawdy humour. It was wildly popular, not only because of the wit and spectacle, but also because it appealed to Restoration politics and was openly supportive of a patriarchal monarchy and, through Trinculo, mocked commonwealth politics.

The Dryden–Davenant play seems to have replaced the original Shakespearean play for some decades. Thomas Shadwell's 1673 operatic version shortened the Dryden–Davenant play further and added elaborate music and scenes. Caliban's role was still diminished. However, yet another operatic version directed by David Garrick in 1757 returned to the First Folio version (in fact the opera was prominently advertised as 'written by Shakespeare') with some pruning and a few additions. The performance ran for nearly 30 years. It continues to be interesting to us as it was first performed at a time when England competed with France for territories in India and the Americas. The result was a more political and race-oriented representation of Caliban. In fact, the frontispiece to one of the editions of the opera text depicts Caliban as a black man swearing allegiance to Trinculo and Stephano.

In 1806, for the first time, John Kemble undertook to stage a more sympathetic reading of Caliban. At this time, commentators such as Coleridge were insisting on 'the monster's' sensitivity and lyricism. Kemble's version (which is an amalgam of Shakespeare's play and Dryden–Davenant's) does not go so far, but staged a Caliban who was not completely coarse or buffoonish in his dialogue delivery and had a touch of the pathetic, if not the tragic. Just as the case of nineteenth-century criticism, the century's staging of *The Tempest* is also very interesting in that it reflects the intellectual, social and political climate of the Victorian age. Generally speaking, nineteenth-century versions were inclined towards extravagant spectacle, something made possible by advances in lighting and sound effects. Coleridge commented on this tendency. While the stage machinery and setting could certainly help to create the illusion, these props troubled Coleridge who believed that 'the principal and only genuine excitement ought to come from within, – from the moved and sympathetic imagination'. With all the excessive special effects on offer, Coleridge feared that the imagination of the spectator would lose its potency. In spite of this disapproval, the fashion of a spectacular *The Tempest* continued unabated. Charles Kean was a well-known Shakespearean producer who spared no expense to create grand, usually historically accurate, costumes and settings. In the case of *The Tempest*, he felt accuracy was less important than creativity. His 1857 version of the play was among the most extravagant witnessed thus far. The opening storm was a spectacle of sound and lighting effects with a rocking galley, the wild shrieks of sailors and the sharp cracking of the ship, the boom of the sea and, amid all this, Ariel darting about the stage surrounded by white globules of fire contrasting with the red glow of lamps. The curtains then dropped as the orchestra played the overture. When the curtains rose again, Prospero was standing on a rock that jutted out over the sea. As the scene between Prospero and Miranda concludes, a flood of sunlight pours over the stage. And so it continues – Ariel's first entrance before Prospero was accompanied by a ball of fire hurled into the stage trap from above, in the banquet scene he was hoisted up in a basket of fruit, Iris rode in on a cloud drawn by doves, an invisible chorus sang at climactic moments and the conclusion was marked by a series of tableaux. All of this spectacle necessarily meant that the actual play text was liberally cut. Most critics praised the production though some felt that the spectacle was excessive and that the acting took second place to the extravagance. However, on the whole, Kean's play set the mode for future nineteenth-century productions, which may not always have been as spectacular, but certainly aspired to be. This trend is interesting as it serves as a reminder of how the language of the play, concrete and vivid as it, has stimulated numerous directors and producers who have felt the need to bring the visual and aural imagery to life on stage. These productions tell us that though *The Tempest* certainly has its philosophical and political dimensions, it is also intensely sensual at the same time. And though Prospero declares that the 'cloud-capped palaces' and other stage spectacles will ultimately dissolve into nothingness, these productions seem to indicate that while this might be the case, the vision, while it exists, is all that spectators possess, and its fleetingness is all the more reason to celebrate it.

Even as the fashion for stage spectacle dominated, there were some interesting developments in the representation of Caliban. As we saw in Chapter 1, the language of the play is ambivalent in its depiction of the 'savage and deformed slave', and the character itself is such a superb creation of poetic language, that it has fired the imaginations of directors and actors. For decades, Caliban was only a monster and every attempt was made to depict a unique and horrifying creature – so Calibans with fishy scales, tangled fur, gnarled tusks and claws, grunted, crawled and roared over stage boards for decades. However, inspired by either Wilson's 'missing link' thesis discussed earlier in this chapter, or by Darwinian theory in general, the actor Frank Benson played Caliban as the 'missing link' in the 1890s. Benson spent hours observing the behaviour and movements of monkeys and apes at the zoo and in a costume that was, as the actor's wife, somewhat wryly perhaps, remarked was, 'half monkey and half coconut', he scampered up and down stage, swarmed up trees and hung off their branches, gibbered and carried a real fish in his mouth (reports say that if this little prop was not changed regularly – and it appears that it often slipped the minds of stage hands – it made for an unpleasant experience for Benson's co-actors and presumably for the star himself). Viewers found this version of Caliban interesting, but the opinion often expressed was that Benson sacrificed the humanity and sensitivity of Caliban in order to emphasize the 'man-monkeyness' and the athleticism that he felt necessarily accompanied that state. However, other Darwin-inspired Calibans did appear on stage, even as late as the mid-twentieth century.

Turn-of-the-century versions of *The Tempest* moved between the spectacular versions favoured in the previous century and simpler stagings. An 1897 production by William Poel's London group was performed in lavish Elizabethan costume, but with relatively minimal scenery and simple background music performed with the pipe and tabor. The production was applauded by reviewers who had tired of the lavish production of the preceding decades and eventually influenced twentieth-century productions. Herbert Beerbohm Tree's 1904 production was a slightly more elaborate one, but avoided the excesses of mid-nineteenth-century productions. Apart from a number of interesting innovations such as the inclusions of brief sections of pantomime, Tree paid attention to what he perceived as Caliban's humanity. He intended that Caliban have a human shape; his costume was made of seaweed and fur, but he also wears a shell necklace, pointing to the human interest in decorating the body. Beerbohm Tree wrote that 'we discern in the soul which inhabits the brutish body of this elemental man the germs of a sense of beauty, the dawn of art'. Tree's production is also interesting in that it had echoes of the imperial theme. In the final tableau, Prospero, Alonso and the rest of the European party are sailing home while Caliban stands alone on the beach and watches the departing ship. He stretches his arms towards it and, as the stage darkens, the last thing the audience sees is Caliban seated on a rock, the lonely king of the island. Tree seems to suggest that the colonized subjects will be sorrowful when the imperial rulers leave, and lost without their civilizing influence. The analogy to colonialism did not escape viewers, and critics took the opportunity to comment on the contemporary situation in Africa and other parts of the world. Interestingly, this Caliban was read by reviewers as standing for the colonized native as well as for the working-class man who has acquired enough education to curse his masters.

*The Tempest* was a popular play through the twentieth century. The monster / missing link Caliban lingered for some decades, but as the century progressed, audiences witnessed more complex, if not more sympathetic renderings of the character. Roger Livesey's 1934 Caliban was actually blacked up for the first time, though as the Vaughans indicate the blackness could in this case 'indicate Caliban's alienness, not necessarily an awareness of racial conflicts'. A 1945 production cast a non-white actor as Caliban for the first time and though the production, by all accounts, did not suggest that Caliban was a victim of colonization, the performance did open the role of Caliban to black actors. Other productions that stand out include Peter Brook's 1968 production in London, which involved an international cast. The version is among the most experimental stage versions of *The Tempest*. In fact, it is more a presentation of the contradictions and abstractions in the text than a literal rendering of the story. At the beginning of the play, the actors faced the audience displaying archetypal emotions. The performance that followed involved a gigantic Sycorax, the grotesque monster-mother from between whose legs Caliban emerges. The staging involved sundry sexual acts performed in pantomime. Brook's version suggests that Caliban does rape Miranda and actually takes over the island, though the plot is not coherent enough to suggest that Brook actually rewrites Shakespeare. The play ends with the epilogue recited in multiple rhythms and inflections after which the audience is left with silence. Brook's film is highly postmodernist, and though it seems to portray a fundamental conflict between innocence and evil, there are no discernible political undertones to it.

Jonathan Miller's 1970 version is distinctly different in this regard. It is remembered today as the first production of *The Tempest* that deliberately highlights the colonial theme. Miller revealed that he was influenced by the post-colonial thinker Octavio Mannoni's ideas (to be discussed briefly later in this chapter) and by the political situation in Nigeria at the time. In fact, the program included an extract from Mannoni's writing and the traditional description of the Caliban character as a 'savage and deformed slave' was removed from the cast of characters. Both Caliban and Ariel were played by black actors. Ariel was depicted as the obedient, somewhat westernized, house servant while Caliban was a field hand. The three goddesses were female black singers. As in the case of postcolonial criticism, there were reviewers who felt that Miller was reading into the play themes that were essentially not in it. However, the review in *Spectator* magazine was more typical. The reviewer stated,

> It will be hard after Mr. Miller's production, ever to see *The Tempest* as the fairytale to which we are accustomed – or indeed to see it any other term than as Shakespeare's account, prosaic and prophetic, of the impact of the Old World on the New: a confrontation which, beginning in amazed delight, moves so swiftly to drawn swords and 'bloody thoughts' that the opening storm seems only a prelude in a minor key to the 'tempest of dissension' that sweeps Prospero's island.

The colonial theme dominated after this and productions hinted at it at the least. In 1970, Ben Kingsley played Ariel as a native servant in a Native American hairpiece. In 1978, David Suchet, who had been cast as Caliban and was told that he'd have to enact a malformed monster, returned to the Shakespeare text and was convinced that Caliban was human and wanted to represent him as a composite of Third World peoples. Some emphasis on colonialism came to be expected and directors were even occasionally rebuked by reviewers in the 1970s and 1980s for not touching on the theme. By the 1980s, Caliban had not only been represented as a black man and an American Indian, but also as working class and a punk rocker. In other words, he had come to stand for multiple groups of marginalized people.

More recently, productions have been varied. Some directors have tired somewhat of the oppressed Caliban and experimented in various ways to emphasize his monstrosity, others have produced variations of the colonial play, while still others have even attempted to evoke the extravagance of the Victorian stagings, or have decided that what's most inspiring about the play is that it is about the making of drama itself and consequently, played up that element. *The Tempest* has been played in different parts of the world: in India, where Ariel has been transformed into the Hindu god Krishna and in Bali, incorporating indigenous shadow puppet theatre and music, to mention just a few examples. Oddly enough, not all post-colonial productions highlight the imperial theme, but the play continues to be staged across the world and is among the works that has made Shakespeare a truly global stage phenomenon.

## *The Tempest* on film

Cinema has always found Shakespearean drama attractive. However, as the Vaughans point out, no popular and relatively faithful cinematic version of *The Tempest* was made till very recently. Film versions that are fairly close to the text tend to be small-budget television shows while the large-screen versions have been mostly loose adaptations of Shakespeare. In fact, the Vaughans add, directors seem to feel that adaptation is the best way to go with *The Tempest* as the play's highly fantastic and magical storyline does not lend itself well to film-making in the realist mode. The first film version was made in 1905, followed by a version in 1911, 1914 and 1921. Several very literal versions followed. The 1956 futuristic fantasy film *The Forbidden Planet*, directed by Fred Wilcox, is an appropriation. It is the year AD 2257 and a Prospero-like figure, one Dr Morbius arrives on a planet named Altair IV by spaceship (of which he is the commander) charged with establishing a colony there. He is accompanied by his wife, who eventually dies leaving him with their daughter Altaira. Morbius stays on, perfecting his skills in technology and exploring the planet, including the remnants of an ancient civilization, the Krell, which existed there several centuries ago. Eventually, a second spaceship looking for Morbius's lost one lands on the planet. The film follows Shakespeare's storyline in some respects (the young John Adams, commander of the second spaceship falls in love with Altaira, for instance). Caliban is not a character in the real sense but a force whose presence is revealed by electromagnetic currents and which occasionally crosses into the spaceship to destroy the humans on it. Towards the end, we are told Caliban is an electrical projection of Dr Morbius's own mind, the destructive primal psychic energy within him, the same energy that destroyed the Krell people many centuries ago. The film ends with Morbius sacrificing his life to destroy Caliban. The planet is destroyed in a thermonuclear reaction while Altaira and her heroic commander escape. Like other post-war science fiction, *The Forbidden Planet* too is filled with a sense of foreboding and terror, including the fear of nuclear power. The film also displays a cynical attitude towards human nature fairly typical of the genre at the time, and, once again, Caliban stands for the dark forces within humanity itself that propel it to carry out large-scale acts of unimaginable cruelty and violence.

Derek Jarman's *The Tempest* (1979) is as experimental as Brook's earlier stage version. The film is set in a crumbling mansion, with Prospero depicted as a mysterious, slightly menacing character to a Caliban played by Jack Berkett, a blind mime actor who depicts Caliban as pathetic rather than villainous, even as he leers at Miranda and spies on her in her bath. The most startling scene is when an adult Caliban nurses at an obese Sycorax's breast. The film appealed to film goers inclined to this mode of cinema who saw it as an original take on Shakespeare's play. Jarman himself said he was trying to create a set that would represent the human mind and its mysterious workings.

Paul Mazursky's 1982 adaptation of the play figures a Prospero-inspired middle-aged American architect Phillip Dimitrious, who leaves his job and wife to go to an isolated Greek island accompanied by his girlfriend Aretha (based on Ariel) and his daughter, Miranda. The island's sole inhabitant is the native, Kalibanos. Eventually, a storm lands on the island a ship bearing Phillip's wife Antonia (clearly drawn from Antonio) and her lover Alonso, who was also Phillip's boss in New York. The language of the film has deliberate echoes of Shakespeare's dialogue and the plot follows Shakespeare's quite closely. The Prospero–Caliban story is not central to the story, but one among the many tensions and conflicts Prospero/Phillip experiences. Mazursky ends his story on a note of reconciliation and harmony, with Phillip reuniting with his wife and apologizing to Kalibanos for his treatment of him. Kalibanos is a comic stereotype of the Third World male – he is alternatively subservient and rude to the Americans, he waits for tourist boats to arrive to make a quick buck, he cons the naive Americans by selling them fake antiques and he lusts for the foreign girl, Miranda. He is not a menacing or tragic figure as in Shakespeare's play. Mazursky finds in *The Tempest* a means to explore themes that are of contemporary interest including midlife crisis and the complexity of modern sexual and marital relationships. His *Tempest* is among the films that continue to be remembered as a Shakespearean adaptation.

Peter Greenaway's 1991 film *Prospero's Books* is an avant-garde rendering of *The Tempest*. The film does not draw attention to the political themes in any obvious way and instead focuses on the magic of writing and the wonders of the imagination. Here, Prospero is played by the famous actor Sir John Gielgud, who also provides the voice to the other parts. Greenaway's film emphasizes the control that Prospero exercises over the events in the island. In fact, Shakespeare's play becomes part of Prospero's fantasy, a piece he is writing. Greenaway focuses on the books in Prospero's library, not only books on magic and monsters, but also books of archaeology, botany, geology, alchemy and architecture. The books are finally drowned in a pool and the characters are released from Prospero's control and can speak for themselves. Prospero returns to Milan and the play he is writing slides into the empty opening pages of Shakespeare's First Folio. Greenaway's film is an unusual viewing experience for those unused to the avant-garde style of film-making, and is a complex film even for those who might be used to the mode, due to its allusions to Renaissance literary culture and history. It is filled with dense, vague but often very beautiful imagery and is quite the visual experience.

Julie Taymour's *The Tempest* (2010) is the most recent film production of the play and can perhaps be described as among the more popular, relatively big-budget versions. Taymour departs from her predecessors' highly experimental versions to the extent that her film follows Shakespeare's script and storyline for the most part. However, she makes one major innovation: Prospero is a woman who has been not only been done out of her title, but was also unfairly accused of witchcraft while in Milan. Taymour's version thus casts the gender politics of the play in new light, though, interestingly, the director does not extend her examination of gender to the depiction of Miranda. Caliban is played by a black African, but apart from the implied racial tension that emerges from this, the colonial dynamic is not particularly highlighted in the film. In fact, it is the Ariel–Prospero relationship that is explored more sensitively. Ariel is beautifully rendered and in many ways is at the centre of the production. The film, like nineteenth-century stage productions, is a delightful visual spectacle with the director making full use of modern digital technology to represent the fantasy world of Shakespeare's play. Apart from the film adaptations briefly surveyed here, there have been a number of other film and television versions of *The Tempest*, primarily made, it seems, for student audiences. Many of them are extremely faithful to the original text barely editing a line; quite a few of them are fairly traditional interpretations and abstain from exploring, for example, the Prospero–Caliban relationship, in any interesting way. *The Tempest* has thus inspired remarkably different styles of film-making.

## Appropriations of *The Tempest*

Caliban's lines 'You taught me language, and my profit on't / Is I know how to curse. The red plague rid you / For learning me your language' (1.2.364–6) have reverberated through the centuries, speaking to peoples and cultures very different from that first audience which witnessed the play. Four hundred years after *The Tempest*, vast numbers of the people who inhabit the globe continue to experience the complex legacy of European imperialism. The languages of the colonial rulers are part of this legacy. Caliban-like, post-colonial subjects have learned to speak in another voice, which they have eventually learnt to make their own. Modern West Indian writer George Lamming sees Caliban's lines on language as among the most powerful in the play, and as eerily prophetic of the way history has unfolded. 'There is no escape from the prison of Prospero's gift', Lamming writes. Prospero's language was used to harass and humiliate the 'savage' of the play, as well as the millions of other Calibans in history. But, 'This gift of language is the deepest and most delicate bond of involvement, it has a certain finality. Caliban will never be the same again. Nor, for that matter will Prospero. Prospero has given Caliban language, and with it an unstated history of consequences, an unknown history of future intentions.' For Lamming, the legacy of language changed Caliban and the course of his history and set him off on a journey to an unknown place; it has also gave him a means to curse, to talk back to Prospero and to speak lines that are profound and poetic.

Real-life Calibans have used Prospero's language to the same purpose: to speak out against colonialism (and other forms of sociopolitical injustice), to assert their claims to their land and to create poetry, fiction and drama. Prospero's language has permeated the fabric of their lives. They have, in other words 'appropriated' the colonial language. Broadly speaking, appropriation is the act of taking something that is not one's own, and claiming ownership over it. This has happened in the case of language in the colonial and post-colonial contexts. Literary appropriation is the act of taking a previously existing work and deliberately revising and rewriting it, often to articulate a very different cultural experience. Writers make no attempt to conceal that they have appropriated an earlier work. On the contrary, they draw attention to the fact and consistently and deliberately remind the reader of the parent text. Writers across the world, most recently and notably, writers from post-colonial societies, have appropriated *The Tempest*. They have rewritten the play and used the act of rewriting to speak out against colonialism, the very same institution that gave them the play and the colonial language. Like Caliban, they too declare, 'You taught me language, and my profit on't / Is I know how to curse'.

So, 'appropriation' is yet another way that *The Tempest* continues to be part of the collective human literary heritage. Shakespeare would probably not have disapproved of these rewritings of his play as his own writing came from the skilful appropriation of literature that he encountered. And perhaps all literary writing is appropriated to some degree. As the modernist poet T. S. Eliot nicely put it, 'Immature poets imitate, mature poets steal, bad poets deface what they take, and good poets make it into something better, or at least something different.' Besides, it is the nature of the original text – its language and other formal elements – that invites or discourages appropriation. Bakhtin in his essay on the dialogic text draws attention to a certain kind of text that is an example of 'authoritarian discourse' – it is 'located in a distanced zone, organically connected to a past that is felt to be hierarchically higher. It is, so to speak, the word of the father'. Any Shakespeare play has certainly been constructed as belonging to the higher echelons of culture, as unchallengeable and inimitable. On the contrary, the very dialogism of a play like *The Tempest*, the competing voices, points of view and ideologies it so tantalizingly offers and withdraws, have made appropriations possible, and even inevitable perhaps. The rewrites that have followed the original *The Tempest* serve as supplements to it: they complete the original as well as alter its meaning and purpose. An awareness of these appropriations will change the way we read the older text. Therefore, in one sense, both the original and the appropriation emerge from each other.

Not all appropriations of *The Tempest* are post-colonial (we should also remember that many of the films discussed in the previous section are also examples of appropriation). In 1864, the English poet Robert Browning borrowed from Shakespeare and composed a poem titled 'Caliban upon Setebos, or Natural Theology in the Island'. *The Tempest* gave Browning an opportunity to reflect on religion and the nature of God at a time when Europe was going through a crisis of faith brought about by Darwinism, the Industrial Revolution and numerous other rapid social changes. Browning's Caliban reflects on the nature of God, who he calls Setebos, the name given to his deity in Shakespeare's play. Caliban cannot understand how this God can be conceived off as anything but arbitrary and unreasonable. He 'hath spite' against Caliban for reasons Caliban does not understand, just as he 'favours Prosper, who knows why?' Browning also satirizes Victorian theologians who believed that man was made in the image of God. If that is the case, says Caliban, God too, like humans, delights for no reason in the suffering of things weaker than him and is arbitrary and cruel and inflicts hurt 'making and marring' humans at will only because they are 'men and merely clay'. And surely, if Prospero is like God, it follows that God is filled with a sense of his own power and is Lord simply 'because he can do what he likes'. Caliban hopes that Setebos/God will vanish some day as 'Warts rub away and sores are cured with slime.' Or perhaps, he will simply be forgotten or turn old and decrepit. However, in spite of this, the poem ends on a note of fear of God/Setebos. What if he has been listening to Caliban's expressions of doubt and ridicule? What if he punishes him like Prospero does? Browning's Caliban, like many other Victorians, is torn between doubt and belief, and the fear that comes with both. Shakespeare's primitive man who can speak becomes the perfect voice through which Browning articulates these thoughts. In fact, the first stanza of the poem begins by acknowledging the power of Caliban's speech. At least when Prospero and Miranda are asleep, Caliban can give his thoughts voice, 'Letting the rank tongue blossom into speech'.

Another, very different nineteenth-century appropriation was by French writer Ernest Renan titled 'Caliban: Suite de *La Tempête*' (1878). Here, Caliban is taken back to Milan by Prospero and educated, but when an unruly mob of common people revolts and takes over the city, Caliban joins them and even becomes their leader. While he eventually does sympathize with Prospero, Caliban, in this piece, becomes a symbol of the dangers of democracy and common rule. A somewhat different message is conveyed by American playwright Percy MacKaye who wrote a masque *Caliban by the Yellow Sands* in 1916 commemorating the anniversary of Shakespeare's death. The masque tried to demonstrate how Caliban, through education and exposure to the gifts of Western civilization, fights against his lust and barbarism, and also rejects his god Setebos and becomes civilized, like Prospero and Miranda. The point of the masque (which proved very popular in its time) was that Caliban (who might stand for other races, or even for the working classes) could be educated and reformed.

The British modernist poet W. H. Auden also turned to *The Tempest*. His long poem *The Sea and the Mirror* (1944) was described as a 'commentary' on *The Tempest* and in the tradition of modernist poetry is interested in the exploration of human psychology. Auden sees Shakespeare's play as exploring the conflict between Ariel (who Auden reads as standing for the human spirit) and Caliban (the bestial). Auden's poem, however, rewrites the Ariel–Caliban relation to indicate that the spiritual and the bestial are both dependent on each other and are inseparable ('Never hope to say farewell', Auden's Ariel tells Caliban), indeed, both are equally flawed as humans are equally imperfect in body, mind and soul. The Prospero of the poem wonders about his post-magic life and is filled with doubt and delusion. Will Miranda be happy, he wonders, 'Will Ferdinand be as fond of a Miranda / Familiar as a stocking?' And what about himself? He even doubts magic; it too ends in disillusion and 'What the books can teach one / Is that most desires end up in stinking ponds.' He also is filled with guilt over Caliban who he describes as his 'impervious disgrace' who is now a wreck 'That sprawls in the weeds and will not be repaired'. The Prospero section also includes a sobering vision of old age. He too, he fears will be 'Just like other old men, with eyes that water / Easily in the wind, and a head that nods in the sunshine / Forgetful, maladroit, a little grubby.' He knows he will die with Caliban's curse in his ear and will 'go knowing and incompetent into my grave'. Antonio also speaks in the poem and makes it clear that he hasn't and will never reform. The poem concludes with a prose monologue from Caliban who addresses Prospero and tells him that he will one day look in the mirror and see Caliban, 'a gibbering, fist-clenched creature . . . the all too solid flesh you must acknowledge as your own'. Prospero realizes that he can never escape Caliban, the primitive and bestial, and also the angry and wounded element that has always been part of him. Once again, *The Tempest* offers a writer located in a different moment in history the means to give voice to the concerns of his age. Auden's poem turns to Shakespeare to articulate the profound disillusionment, angst and weariness experienced in World War II Europe.

Shakespeare is an important part of the school and university curriculum in those societies that experienced English colonization. In fact, it has been argued that English literature, including Shakespeare, was one of the instruments colonialists deliberately turned to in order to create the ideal colonial subject, English speaking, but still submissive, who would feel the required reverence for English culture. In today's post-colonial world, the place and significance of Shakespeare is possibly more complex and is as rapidly changing as these societies are. Writers and other artists from these cultures feel a paradoxical sense of distance as well as identification with 'The Bard'. However, Shakespeare's plays, especially *The Tempest*, have long been a popular choice for colonized and post-colonial artists to appropriate and make their own.

Not all of these appropriations are literary works. The Uruguayan philosopher José Enrique Rodó wrote his essay *Ariel* in the early 1900s where he used Caliban as symbol for the United States. Latin Americans at the time were concerned about the imperialist ambitions of the United States over the rest of the Americas. The 'yanquis' thus became, for Rodó, a type of Caliban, ugly, aggressive and greedy. The Latin Americans themselves, he said, should strive to be a kind of Ariel, cultured, sensitive, seeking art, beauty, truth and freedom. For another thinker, the psychologist Octavio Mannoni, Shakespeare's play offered a model for and a vocabulary to explain his ideas on the psychological causes and effects of the political phenomenon that is colonialism. His book, *Prospero and Caliban: The Psychology of Colonization* (1950, first translated in English in 1964) was an attempt to explain the political situation in Madagascar, which was a French colony. Prospero and Caliban are used as metaphors for the colonizer and colonized. For Mannoni, colonialism comes about and is advanced because of an inferiority complex on the part of Prospero who therefore feels the need to overcompensate and establish himself as an aggressor and ruler and a 'dependence complex' on the part of Caliban who is childlike and wants to be taken care of and ruled over, even though this might result in his humiliation. Shakespeare's play offered Mannoni the means to articulate his ideas, ideas which have been criticized by later post-colonial thinkers who not only saw Mannoni's position on the 'Caliban complex' as incorrect, but as dangerous in that it could potentially discourage peoples struggling for their political rights. However, Mannoni's book spurred quite a few other writers to turn to *The Tempest* in order to explore their own experiences of colonialism

In 1960, George Lamming, a writer from the Barbados, wrote *The Pleasures of Exile*, which was a critical reading of *The Tempest* and which also used the play as an occasion to produce meditations on the collective history of the Caribbean and on his own personal history in which he projected himself as a Caliban figure in dialogue with Prospero. Lamming wishes, he writes, 'to make use of *The Tempest* as a way of presenting a certain state of feeling which is the heritage of the exiled and colonial writer from the Caribbean'. The book was written at a time when little criticism or history was produced from outside Euro-American centres, and when critics rarely drew attention to their own sociocultural position. Lamming comments on how Caliban's humanity is reduced by imperialism and he becomes 'an occasion, a state of existence which can be appropriated and exploited for the purposes of another's development'. He especially focuses on Caliban as a slave, a designation that especially struck the author as, 'I am a direct descendent of slaves, too near the actual enterprise to believe that its echoes are over with the reign of emancipation'. But Lamming complicates his position. He also realizes that Caliban is also 'a direct descendent of Prospero'. Not only has he, the colonized, been shaped by his engagement with the colonial master, both of them have been marked by the imperial experience and both of them are exiles. Lamming especially focuses on the issue of the education of Caliban. The most significant parallels between the play and Caribbean history are in this respect and it is because of colonial education and the teaching and learning of English that the Caribbean writer is most drawn to the play. He, Lamming, will use this legacy 'not to curse our meeting – but to push it further, reminding the descendants of both sides that what's done is done, and can only be seen as a soil from which other gifts, or the same gift endowed with different meanings, may grow towards the future which is colonized by our acts'. Lamming uses *The Tempest* to project his hopes for the future of his country (which was not yet independent at the time he wrote his book) and for the world in general, a harmonious future that he hopes both Prospero and Caliban will work towards.

*The Tempest* was used by other post-colonial thinkers to reflect on their political situations. In 1971, the Cuban writer Roberto Fernandez Retamar wrote a book titled *Caliban* in which he rejected Rodó's identification with Ariel and said that Caliban was the most appropriate symbol for the Caribbean people. In a famous line, Retamar declares, 'I know no metaphor more expressive of our cultural situation, of our reality . . . What is our history, what is our culture, if not the history and culture of Caliban?' For Retamar, Caliban was not only the oppressed slave and subject of imperialism, he was also the voice that challenged it, the rebel who gave real-life colonized peoples hope and reason to fight against the injustices imposed on them.

Apart from these political and philosophical works, a number of literary appropriations of *The Tempest* have emerged. The best known of these is by Aimé Césaire from Martinique whose 1969 play *A Tempest*, originally in French (titled *Une Tempête*) has been widely translated, studied and enacted around the world. *A Tempest* is an overtly political protest play and Césaire is especially inspired by Negritude, a political movement whose aim was to create a global black identity based on origins in the African continent and pride in black heritage. The Antonio–Alonso thread of the plot is marginalized in *A Tempest* and the central conflict is between Prospero and a black Caliban, who is definitely the heroic centre of the piece and cast as the oppressed but defiant slave and colonial subject. The play links Caliban with the African American civil rights activist Malcolm X and with Kenyan freedom fighters (in fact, Caliban uses the word 'Uhuru', the Swahili cry for freedom). He celebrates his mother, denies the accusation of rape (unlike Shakespeare's Caliban) insists on speaking his native language and even refuses to be called 'Caliban'. The play is a psychodrama, a battle of wills and emotions, fought between the justly resentful exploited (Caliban) and the power-hungry exploiter (Prospero), the person who is imaginative, vibrant and in tune with nature (Caliban) and one who is the coldly rational and mechanical (Prospero). Ariel is viewed by Caliban as the obedient servant to Prospero who 'sucks up' to him and faithfully executes his orders with a despicable 'Uncle Tom's patience'. Many of Shakespeare's lines are visible in Césaire's work (although Césaire mostly prefers a direct, hard-hitting prose) as are some of the structural elements. Césaire chooses to interrupt the masque of Greek goddesses with the entrance of the impudent Yoruba (West African) phallic god Eshu who mocks Prospero and drives him into a rage. At the conclusion of *A Tempest*, both Prospero and Caliban are left together on the island in terrible intimacy. As Prospero puts it, 'And now, Caliban, it's you and me!'. But the play indicates that it does not end well for Prospero. He appears in the last scene 'aged and weary. His gestures are jerky and automatic, his speech is weak, toneless and trite.' In spite of his defiant cry 'But I shall stand firm . . . I shall not let my work perish! I shall protect civilization!', he also realizes that nature in its powerful fecundity has taken over the island again, and 'In the distance, above the sound of the surf and the chirping of birds, we hear snatches of Caliban's song: FREEDOM HI-DAY, FREEDOM HI-DAY!'. Here is no Caliban slinking away to 'seek for grace'. For Césaire, as for most post-colonial writers, it is crucial to end on this note of hope and with a vision of freedom, however distant it might have seemed at the moment of writing.

Some post-colonial poetry has also been inspired by *The Tempest*. Kamau Brathwaite another Caribbean writer, begins his poem 'Caliban' (1969) by listing momentous dates in Caribbean history, including Columbus's arrival in 1492. The poem echoes Shakespeare's Caliban's line 'Ban-ban Caliban':

> And
> Ban
> Ban
> Cali-
> Ban
> Like to play
> Pan
> At the Carni-
> Val

Caliban here is transformed into the iconic steel-band player and 'limbo' dancer of Caribbean carnival who plays and dances to protect himself from Prospero and also to exuberantly celebrate his cultural heritage. Recognizing the connection between language and power in the colonized world, a dynamic that is illustrated so well in *The Tempest*, Brathwaite has consistently promoted the literary potential of the creoles of the Caribbean, choosing himself to write in what he calls 'nation language' rather than standard English. In another poem 'Letter Sycorax', he has Caliban writing to his mother:

> *Dear mamma*
> i writin yu dis letter/ *wha*
> guess what! Pun a computer o/kay? (emphasis in original)

In this and other poems, Brathwaite takes the notion of 'nation language' further and chooses to experiment on the computer with font size, capitalization, punctuation and layout, resulting in a dynamic, unconventional poetry that defies standard English, and which he dubs 'Sycorax Video Style' in honour of Caliban's mother.

The African poet Lemuel Johnson has written '*Highlife for Caliban*' in 1973 in which he uses the rhythms of African speech and West Indian song to write a collection of poems that is part dirge and part celebration of Caliban. Caliban not only laments his own birth, he is a thing that is 'black, lacking / in air that is light', but also articulates the hopes and desires felt by him, his dream of being 'elf with printless foot'. The poem ends on a note of hope. One day, when the revels end, Caliban will be ready 'to wake and cry to dream again'.

Jyotsna Singh has argued that while many post-colonial appropriations, including Césaire's play, have examined the Prospero–Caliban relationship in original ways, they still continue to see both colonization and the struggle for political freedom as an exclusively male enterprise. The women of the play have received little to no attention from these writers, and ironically, they have made out gender issues to be at odds with other kinds of political struggle rather than part of the same endeavour. It has largely been left to the women writers who have appropriated *The Tempest* to emphasize the play's female characters. Some of these writers have even tried to look at colonization and gender in relation to each other.

The American poet Hilda Doolittle, known as H. D., is one of the founders of the Imagist school of poetry. A poetic tribute to Shakespeare titled 'By Avon River' was written in 1949 after a visit to Stratford-upon-Avon. The fairly long poem includes a section on *The Tempest* and is interesting because it is one of the few appropriations of the play in which Claribel, the daughter of Alonso is the focus. 'We know little of *the king's fair daughter / Claribel*', writes H. D (emphasis in original). The mysterious Claribel's story came before the story of *The Tempest*, she is missing from the play itself: 'Read for yourself, *Dramatis Personae*, . . . Read through again, *Dramatis Personae*; / She is not there at all.' Claribel, however, continues to haunt the poet, the birds shrill her name and 'Claribel echoes from this rainbow-shell, / I stooped just now to gather from the sand.' H. D.'s poem not only makes us think about a character merely mentioned in passing, but it also makes us wonder about the missing Claribel's story. We are first told (in Shakespeare's play) that hers was 'a sweet marriage' (2.1.73) and then later informed that she was a reluctant bride, torn between 'loathness and obedience', forced into marrying a foreign groom (2.1.131). The poem makes us wonder how it turned out for her, Claribel, Queen of Tunis. The poet does not attempt to speculate, but she appears to identify with the voiceless Claribel, and the reminder that the Shakespeare play did not see the story of this young woman as worth pursuing, stands in tension with H. D.'s reverence and admiration for Shakespeare and her awareness that she has inherited the literary heritage of which he is the centrepiece. Later in the poem, the poet does find a way a way to articulate her thoughts, an opportunity never given to Claribel.

The Caribbean-born author Marina Warner turns to the figure of Miranda in her novel *Indigo* (1992). Miranda is a young woman born in the island of St. Kitts (like Warner herself) who is part English and part Creole. Warner's novel moves between the present and the past when the island was settled by Miranda's English ancestor, Sir Christopher Everard. Miranda is a photographer who struggles to find a subject for her art, even as she realizes it would be impossible, in the context of the island, to create an art divorced of history and politics. She eventually marries a black actor who performs Caliban and bears a daughter who seems to embody the future. Warner also makes Sycorax, represented as a native wise woman and sorceress, an active presence in the novel. She uses *The Tempest* to explore the multicultural and multiracial society of the Caribbean that struggles with its traumatic history of colonization and slavery. Like H. D., Warner too uses one of Shakespeare's female characters to approach the theme of the female artist struggling to come into her own. Like other female authors, she finds that she has to confront, engage with and appropriate the iconic male author even as she strives to find her own voice.

The India-born Canadian poet Suniti Namjoshi's 1989 sequence of poems 'Snapshots of Caliban', moves between different voices and explores the relationship between Miranda, Caliban and Prospero. In Prospero's meditation, Caliban is a girl, a girl who Prospero cannot understand:

> There's something wrong with Caliban.
>      Is it her shape? Is it her size?
> If I could say that Caliban is stupid,
> then that might help, but she can read and write
>      and sometimes her speech is so lucid.

Prospero moves between bewilderment, exasperation (Caliban, he complains, howls like 'some tiresome animal') and fear. He is apprehensive about Caliban's dreams, 'For there is something / I dislike so thoroughly about Caliban: / if she had her way, she would rule the island, / and I will not have it'. Namjoshi combines here the fear of the foreign Caliban with the fear of the woman Caliban. Animal, foreign and female at the same time, Caliban becomes that onto which Prospero projects his deepest anxieties. Another section of the poem titled 'From Caliban's Notebook' Caliban says that the entire story was a dream, there was no tempest, no landing ship, Miranda ('M') dreamt up her young prince and Prospero ('P') dreamt that he had taken revenge for the wrongs done to him. And, at the end, no one left the island: 'And they never got away, / for here we all are, M and myself / and doddering P, still islanded / still ailing, looking seaward / for company'. In Namjoshi's version, Caliban seems to have some insight into things that the others lack, lost as they are in their worlds of fantasy, and the poet uses him to explore the complexities of gender identities and relationships.

Other works can also be described as feminist appropriations of *The Tempest*. Virginia Mason Vaughan identifies novels such as the Canadian writer Margaret Laurence's *The Diviners* (1974) and the African American writer Gloria Naylor's novel *Mama Day* (1989) as instances of women writers revising the play, and there might be more novels, poems and plays that belong to the category. As discussed in Chapter 1, the women in the play are scarcely there in it, but their presence, such as it is, can be subject to varying interpretation, and potential writers could still mine the play further to find ways to articulate their own interests and concerns.

So, *The Tempest* has become a play for all peoples and all time. Some would argue that these literary appropriations, and even the critical readings that have emerged over the centuries, are not true to the play at all, that they distort the original work, which also remains the only one with any real merit. But for many creative writers, and for critics and directors as well, *The Tempest* can never be finished, it yields further stories and defies attempts to finalize its meaning. That is what makes it a living text. Even for those who may not be particularly interested in the appropriations themselves, or in certain kinds of critical readings, it is important to realize that engaging with a variety of reworkings and interpretations still impacts the way we respond to the original play.

# Writing matters

## *Criticism*

The criticism that you were introduced to in this chapter demonstrates that *The Tempest* is a remarkably complex play and when viewed from different perspectives yields a range of readings. Learning more about the different traditions of critical reception – formalism, historicism, feminism, post-colonialism and so forth – will enhance your own critical skills. For one thing, the recognition that every critic comes from one perspective or another will help you deal with the critical essays you will encounter when you begin to do research on the play. Much has been written and published on *The Tempest* and it is easy to be confused and overwhelmed by all the critical material. Placing different critical essays alongside each other will help you understand whether and how they differ from each other and the value of each piece of critical work. The knowledge that critics have their own distinct methodologies and assumptions will help you categorize the critical material and even help you comprehend better what each individual essay is trying to accomplish. It will benefit your own writing as you find yourself getting more interested in certain theories and methodologies.

It is important to realize that *all* readers have theories of literature. Each time we pass value judgment on a book or a film, we are bringing into play certain assumptions about what makes for an interesting narrative. Similarly, every school or theory of criticism asks certain fundamental questions (*What is literature? What does it do? What is the link between literature and reality? What makes a 'good' narrative?*) and answers them differently. Every school of criticism also asks its own distinct questions and raises its own issues. For example, feminist criticism asks about representations of gender in literature and formalism is interested in investigating the workings of literary form and literary language. Acquainting and affiliating yourself with one critical trend or another, depending on your interests, and also after making sure that that particular critical perspective is suitable for the play, will help you find focus as you write about *The Tempest*. You will understand how you cannot say everything about the play. You have to ask one or two related questions about it and attempt to answer them in your own essay. These critical traditions also have different ideas of what constitutes evidence – for the formalist, any observation about a text must be backed up by pointing to elements within the text only, whereas the historicist goes outside the text and looks for evidence in history and other historical documents. As you find yourself drawn to one critical tradition or another, you will develop a good sense of how to back up your own critical claims.

Even as we talk of distinct critical traditions or different theories of literature, we should remember that these are not watertight categories in practice. The best kind of criticism borrows from different approaches. For example, feminist critics can draw upon formalism to explicate the text or can fold post-colonial issues and concerns into their work. It is also important to remember that good criticism is never entirely predictable. Even when you take on a feminist or post-colonial stance you should not simply echo the most obvious statements that a critic affiliated with either of these schools might make on the play.

Attempt to answer the following questions either individually or in groups. They will give you the opportunity to reflect further on your assumptions about literature and literary criticism in general, or on criticism of *The Tempest* in particular:

**1** According to some critics, literature's function is mainly *poetic*. This implies that it is primarily a work of art and its most important function is aesthetic. Others would say that literature is *mimetic*, that is, it reflects reality or engages with the world outside of itself in some way. Draw up arguments that would support both the poetic and mimetic schools of thought. Then think about where you stand in this debate. Do you think that *The Tempest*'s mimetic function is more important and obvious than its poetic or vice versa?

2  Do you feel that 'modern' critical approaches like feminism and post-colonialism are not really based on the play itself, but are dictated by our own contemporary concerns and sensitivities? Discuss.

3  Is it important for you as a critic, to know what intentions and meanings Shakespeare had in mind as he wrote *The Tempest*? How would this knowledge (assuming you had access to it) impact your own interpretation of the play?

4  Choose two critics who seem to have radically different things to say about *The Tempest* and write a short dialogue in which they converse with each other about the play and how they read it. Make sure you read their essays before starting this exercise.

5  Imagine you were interviewing one of the critics mentioned in this chapter. Read his or her essay and draw up a list of five questions you would ask him or her. The questions should be intended to help you understand the critic's methodology and interpretation better.

6  Assume that you are doing a feminist reading of the play focusing on Sycorax or a reading of class tensions in the play that focuses on Stephano's and Trinculo's roles. As we have pointed out, all good readings are rooted in the language of the play. Pick out relevant and interesting sections from the play that you could use in your analysis.

7  You are interested in writing about one element of the play, its setting. How do you think a formalist critic would write about the setting of *The Tempest*? What are the most important points he or she would make? Similarly, think about how either a historicist critic or a post-colonial critic would construct an argument about the play's setting.

## *Film and stage versions*

Writing about *The Tempest* on film and stage is also a way of critically engaging with the play text. You could simply pick a film version or watch a local stage production and write a review where you summarize and evaluate the performance, or you could write a longer critical essay on the play or film. It is important that you don't simply point out differences between the printed and staged / filmed version because there are bound to be several. However, you need to consider the director's vision of the play as an interpretation of it and comment accordingly. You should also use the film or staged performance to examine the current meaning and value of Shakespeare in general and *The Tempest* in particular.

You could also attempt more brief writing exercises using these prompts. They will also give you the opportunity to think about the choices that directors and actors need to make.

**1** You are casting executive for a new film version of *The Tempest*. Which contemporary actor would you choose to play Prospero, Caliban, Miranda and Ariel? Explain your choices with references to the actor's skills, physicality and other roles he/she has played.

**2** You are asked to create a soundtrack to a film version of *The Tempest*. Select five songs/pieces of music for five scenes. List each title, artist and scene and explain your choice.

## *Appropriation*

Writing about appropriation means engaging with the inevitable 'intertextuality' of all writing. It is acknowledging, in the words of Michel Foucault that 'The frontiers of a book are never clear-cut . . . it is caught up in a system of references to other books, other texts, other silences, it is a node in a network.' However, even as we do not privilege the autonomy of the text and approach both the play and its rewrites as belonging to a complex field of discourse, Foucault also reminds us to acknowledge a text's uniqueness, its distinct characteristics. We also need to ask, he says, 'how is it that one particular statement appeared rather than another?' Writing about appropriations is therefore a way of responding to *The Tempest* and also engaging fully with another text and another literary tradition. Even if you are primarily interested in Shakespeare's play and would like it to constitute the focal point of your essay and are using the appropriation only for purposes of comparison, it is important that you know the appropriation and the tradition or body of work it emerges from well. For example, if you are including Césaire's *A Tempest* in your essay, you need to know not only Shakespeare's play, but also Césaire's work and something about the literary traditions of the Francophone Caribbean and Black Theatre of the 1960s. It would be unfair to Césaire's play and make for a shoddy critical essay if you simply analysed the revised work as any other version of *The Tempest*. Studying appropriations is also a way of thinking about Shakespeare's impact on other cultures and literatures, as well as the institution of Shakespeare, its significance and cultural value in a global context. Here are a few questions that will help you reflect further about appropriation and also give you an opportunity to rewrite *The Tempest* yourself:

1 Do you agree with T. S. Eliot's statement quoted in page 150 of this chapter that all writing is basically rewriting?

2 More specifically, do you think appropriations of *The Tempest* lack originality and are of less interest than the original (please read some of the literary appropriations for yourself, do not rely on the brief comments offered in this chapter).

**3**  If you were rewriting the play, who would be the character you would sympathize with and make the play's centre: Prospero, Caliban, or one of the other characters? Would you change the conclusion of the play?

**4**  Each of the writers discussed in the section on appropriation in this chapter is responding to a specific aspect of the play: the binaries that inform its structure, the ambiguities of the language, the things implied but left unsaid. If you were rewriting *The Tempest* what kind of new piece would you produce: a poem, a short story, another play, even a song lyric (if so, which music genre)? What features of the play stand out for you and prompt your choice?

**5**  Select a scene from the play and write it as a song lyric for a specific music genre (e.g. folk ballad, rap, nu metal, punk, pop song or classical opera).

**6**  Take the main characters with all their emotional and social characteristics and write a short story with the characters placed in a completely different time and setting.

# CHAPTER FOUR

# Writing and language skills

While we think of plays, poems and fiction as instances of the fine use of language, we are inclined to assume that critical essays on these works are rather unexciting and drab. It is important, however, to realize that critical analysis also involves original and creative thinking, as well as skilful writing. A good piece of criticism should be interesting to read and should offer new insights into the text and, ideally, into the nature of language itself.

As a student of the play, you will be required to complete a range of writing exercises, each of which will call upon slightly different skills. We have glanced at some of these – short responses, free writing exercises, reviews, exercises based on closer reading – in the 'Writing matters' sections that followed each chapter. Whatever the assignment, you should draw mainly from the material and ideas the play itself yields and also strengthen your responses by turning to your instructor's comments and insights and those of your classmates. You might occasionally find yourself answering an exam on *The Tempest*. Responses to examination questions call upon a specific set of skills. While preparing for an exam you will, obviously, make sure you know the play well and study your notes on it. You should also anticipate the questions you might be asked. A good way to go about this is to rephrase points about the play you have in your notes as questions. This will help you get a good sense of the range and variety of potential questions. As most exams involve questions that require relatively short responses (ranging from a paragraph to a short essay), it is also good to practice writing precisely and quickly. It is also crucial to answer the question asked. While this might be stating the obvious, exam takers often do not directly respond to the questions posed to them. For example, a question such as 'What is Ariel's role in *The Tempest*?', often sees the respondent going off on a tangent, focusing on peripheral matters or summarizing Ariel's story. A more productive way of approaching this question would be to comment on the ways in which Ariel highlights certain aspects of other characters' personalities (his 'delicacy' vs Sycorax's cruelty and Caliban's brutality), to examine the ways in which he complicates the issues of slavery and liberty (What kind of slave is he? Why does he want his master to love him?) or to write about his complex relationship with Prospero. Since you have limited time to complete the examination, your response should be concise and selective.

As we go further into the era of the World Wide Web, there are a number of other less conventional writing exercises that you could engage in. You could participate in an online discussion forum set up on the play by an instructor. As you read and research the play, you could also maintain a blog on it and open it up for your classmates and even the general public to comment on (there are hundreds of thousands of Shakespeare fans out there and at least some of them are bound to stumble upon and comment on your blog, especially if it is interesting enough). Writing a 'wiki' on topics such as 'Shakespeare', 'Shakespearean Romance', '*The Tempest*', '*The Tempest* on Film' or 'Caliban', is also an engaging exercise. A 'wiki' (in the manner of all 'Wikipedia' entries) is a short online essay to which additions and other changes can be made by others. One student would begin the wiki and others would serve as editors. The final product would be the result of the cumulative thinking of all students. It is even possible to set up a website on *The Tempest* or a Facebook page on it. The advantage of online exercises is that they are often collaborative and call for a writing style that is accessible and precise, even as it is elegant. Online exercises also make it possible to use different media (visuals, film clips, audio clips of readings of the play along with the written word) to communicate your responses to the play.

# Writing a critical analysis essay on *The Tempest*

While the possibilities are endless, most students will still find themselves writing the conventional critical analysis paper. Traditional as it might be, the critical essay is an excellent exercise in that it calls for a deep engagement with the play and with the critical materials on it; it tests your reading, analytical and interpretative skills, as well as your ability to write well.

A critical essay is not distinct from the shorter writing exercises that you have ideally been working on as you study the play. It builds on these shorter responses and reflections. The brief pieces of writing on close reading or explication that you have completed are especially useful as you embark on the critical analysis paper. The explication exercises had you working closely with the language of the play and a good critical essay, whatever the topic and argument, is built on a similar engagement. You might be writing on a topic such as 'Aural imagery in *The Tempest*' or on 'The Nature of Colonial power in *The Tempest*' and although, the latter topic (or both topics for that matter) might not appear to deal directly with issues of language, it is crucial to remember that the play is fundamentally a linguistic artefact and *nothing* intelligent or interesting can be said about it unless you recognize this and look closely at its language. Transitioning from shorter to longer writing assignments is not about leaving the former behind and moving on to something lengthier and somehow more sophisticated, but involves building on the understanding about the play gained from the shorter pieces of writing. Conversely, writing a critical essay paper is not simply about expanding a piece of explication, review or other shorter response. A critical essay has its own purpose and structure.

## *The topic and the argument*

A critical essay involves writing about one particular aspect of the play. It also involves stating and proving an argument or thesis about a specific topic. Choosing a topic to write on is your first step. A play like *The Tempest* is so rich and so complex that it yields a number of topics. While this is certainly preferable to a text that yields very little, it is easy to get overwhelmed by the large number of possibilities before you. You could write about the island setting, about Prospero, about magic, about the women in the play, about appropriations of the play, about all or some of these in relation to each other – the options seem endless. A way of narrowing down is to re-read the play and your notes and jot down ideas till you identify one that seems interesting (crucial if you are going to be putting in the time and effort that a critical essay demands), doable in the time you have to complete the essay, also keeping the length of the assignment in mind. As you read the play for potential topics, read keeping both form *and* content in mind. Don't just look for the ideas and themes the play communicates ('gender', 'colonial power', 'old age', etc.), but also keep in mind the formal aspects of the play that foreground and further these topics. Take special note of formal patterns, contradictions and ambiguities, as interesting questions about the play emerge from these.

Even if you are writing a relatively long paper, a narrower topic will make it possible to do justice to whatever it is you are writing about. So, for example, '*The Tempest* as reflecting central concerns of the Renaissance' is a topic that can be ruled out right away. How many aspects of the Renaissance (the sea voyages/magic/issues of political succession/gender) can you expect to cover in a single paper, or even in a book for that matter? Instead, your topic could be just one of these aspects. Let's say you identify the following topics as interesting and worthwhile:

- Magic in *The Tempest*
- The island setting of *The Tempest*
- Characters' names in *The Tempest*
- Music in *The Tempest*
- The nature of political power in *The Tempest*

These topics are doable, but still fairly broad and you should work to focus further. What you need to do is to arrive at an argument or a thesis. While the topic indicates what your paper will focus on, the argument is what you have to say about the topic. It is the position you, as a reader of the play, are going to take on the topic. While the word 'argument' seems to imply an aggressive exchange between individuals, and it might even seem rather odd to argue about literature, it is useful to remember that literary texts are, in one sense, arguments in and of themselves, setting forward and complicating opinions on different issues. *The Tempest*, as we've seen, does this on themes ranging from colonialism to the nature of magic. Besides, a good argument is never an ugly exchange. On the contrary, it involves the ability to convince listeners of the validity of your point of view, an art that the ancient Greeks termed 'rhetoric'. An essay in which you state and prove an argument about the play will demonstrate your ability to use clear and persuasive rhetoric.

In order to arrive at a thesis, it is often a good idea to reshape your topic as a question, preferably a question with various debatable answers. So, just the topic on magic listed above yields a number of questions (think about the questions you could ask in relation to the other topics listed):

- Is Prospero's magic a benign or dark force in the play?
- Why does the play move towards Prospero renouncing his magic?

- How does Prospero's magic change as a result of his stay on the island?
- What kind of power does magic give Prospero?

The answer to these questions would constitute a thesis or argument:

- Prospero's magic is ultimately a dark force in the play.
- The play moves towards the renunciation of magic as Prospero learns to become less egoistical and domineering.
- The play demonstrates how magic becomes associated with political power as a result of Prospero's stay on the island.

Of course, you will find that not all these arguments are particularly interesting or profound, or that you don't have too much to say on them. If that is the case, you should not hesitate to reject the argument and start over. A good argument is interesting and bold, it is also debatable – it should be possible for another reader to disagree with it. This wouldn't be the case if it is too obvious (*'Prospero derives his power from magic'* or *'The play ends very differently for each of Prospero's servants – Ariel is free while Caliban is not'*, are examples of arguments that state the obvious or simply point out an aspect of the plot that almost no reader would have missed). As your ability to read and interpret the play develops, your arguments will become increasingly complex and sophisticated. But even if you are fairly new to writing a critical essay you should try to develop and complicate your arguments. For instance, a careful examination of the language of the play and a sensitive reading of its ambiguities and contradictions will help you reframe the relatively simple arguments above:

- Prospero's magic is ultimately a dark force in the play. This makes him somewhat similar to Sycorax even as he tries to distance himself from her. This complicates his status as hero.

● The play ends with the renunciation of magic, but Prospero only exchanges it for more earthly kinds of power – both moral and political – at the end of the play.

● The play demonstrates how knowledge of magic becomes associated with political power and the capacity to subjugate others after Prospero's arrival on the island. In this, it is reminiscent of how European technologies and scientific knowledge were used to control the natives of colonized territories.

● Magic gives Prospero the ability to control other characters through physical violence, but more often through the ability to shape their thoughts and to enchant them through visual display. In this, it is similar to the power of the theatre.

You should be able to state your argument in a sentence or two. Clarity is crucial. Very often, thesis statements are vague and garbled. However, don't sacrifice complexity for clarity – a sweeping generalization might be very clear, but it rarely makes for an interesting argument. Finally, an argument is contestable, it needs to be proved, which is where you need to line up the evidence.

## *Evidence*

Although, the organization of the critical essay demands that you begin by stating the argument early in the paper and follow it up with several pages devoted to proving it, the fact is that the argument emerges from the evidence; you cannot come up with an argument about the play that appeals to you and tailor the evidence or manipulate the text to support it. Besides, the evidence you use to support your argument will depend on some of the assumptions you make about literary texts, in other words your 'literary theory'. You might decide, in the tradition of formalism, that the best and only evidence should come from the play itself. Or you might decide that the context that is most relevant to understanding *The Tempest* is the entire body of Shakespeare's plays (or you might narrow it down to the comedies, or the romances, or the last few plays). Alternatively, you might be convinced by the historicist method and want to draw on knowledge about the historical moment and to other non-literary historical documents to support your evidence.

Examine the text closely for textual evidence and assemble it all together. While the storyline does constitute evidence (e.g. if your topic is Miranda's status in the play you need to take into account the fact that she falls in love with Ferdinand), more valuable evidence comes from the language used by the playwright to convey the fact of their love (How does Ferdinand address her? How does Prospero talk about the love that blossoms between the young people? What language does Miranda use to express desire?). This is where your close-reading skills become very useful. The structure of the plot (the 'story' is simply what happens, while 'plot' is the author's deliberate arrangements of events in the narrative) can also constitute evidence (again, if you are talking about Miranda, you could consider why the plot delays her engagement with Ferdinand). Never ignore evidence that contradicts your argument. For instance, you might be arguing that Miranda is the submissive daughter, but there is plenty in the play to suggest that she is quite assertive in her own way. You will need to take this into account in order to respond to any obvious challenge to your argument and also to complicate it. Once you feel you have your textual evidence together, evaluate it. Make sure you are not using evidence to support an obvious point, such as a narrative fact (you don't need to quote from the play to let your reader know that Miranda was an infant when she came to the island or that she is to be engaged to Ferdinand at the end) or use too much evidence to support a fairly minor point you are making.

If you are turning to historical context or to other historical documents for evidence, you should keep in mind that this is always in addition to evidence from the play. Besides, use those aspects of contexts that seem relevant and useful. There is no point in beginning your paper with a general overview of the Renaissance, or even in stating a few interesting facts about the time period unless they are of relevance to your topic and argument. It is true that a lot of New Historicist criticism begins by talking about some aspect of Renaissance history that seems completely unconnected to the play, but very soon into the critical essay the connection is established and the relevance of the opening made clear. You should keep in mind that the historical evidence supplements the textual evidence; *the play* always stands at the centre of your paper.

## *Research*

Even simply reading a Shakespeare play might entail additional research. If the notes in your text are inadequate, you will find yourself turning to a good dictionary such as the *Oxford English Dictionary* to look up the meaning and etymology of words. An authoritative encyclopaedia such as the *Britannica* will provide you additional information on background and references. A good handbook of literary terms is also useful to help you know and clearly define the various figures of speech and to provide you brief introductions to the literary genres.

In the course of writing on *The Tempest*, you will need to do further research. You will turn to additional sources to find additional information on the historical context and to read up critical essays on the play. While an encyclopaedia is a good place to start looking up information on, say King James's rule or the New World voyages of the sixteenth and seventeenth centuries, you should eventually turn to advanced scholarship on the time period. Scholarship on Renaissance literature is often interdisciplinary and most often history is the discipline turned to in order to assist in the critical analysis of literature of the time period. As in the case of criticism, historians come from certain traditions of scholarship, will have their own biases, and highlight certain aspects of context and downplay others. You will soon become aware of this and learn to use more than one source to get a range of interpretations on historical events surrounding the play. While no topic in history is entirely uncontroversial, it is even more important to read multiple and varied sources on topics that have provoked scholarly debate, such as the African slave trade, or European–Native American relations in colonial Virginia. While advanced critical work requires that you turn to primary historical documents, even a less advanced level paper will benefit from incorporating analyses of contextual documents. Many editions of *The Tempest* reprint some of these along with the play, so it shouldn't be too difficult for you to lay hands on excerpts from the narratives on the Bermuda voyages or from Montaigne's essay 'Of Cannibals'. As your topic gets more sophisticated, you will need to look for relevant documents in the archives. Often fresh insights into the play are offered by pairing it with documents that are not widely known, or whose relevance to the play has not been brought to light before. You need not read the play as a historical document, that is, you do not need to claim that it reflects the truth of the historical moment; instead, you can think about how it comes into conversation with the 'real' in a variety of ways, ranging from confirming, to challenging, to influencing it.

Incorporating what other critics have said on the play will inevitably enhance the quality of your essay. You will never be the first person to write on any Shakespeare play. Your essay should demonstrate that you realize that you are always part of an ongoing conversation. The fact that there has been so much written on Shakespeare's plays, especially a play as popular as *The Tempest*, makes the task of finding criticism both easier and more difficult. Easier because you are never going to run short of essays to read on the play, difficult because there is an overwhelming amount of material available and you need to evaluate it in order to arrive at the essays that are relevant to your topic. As mentioned in the 'Writing matters' section of Chapter 3, understanding the critical tradition that scholars come from makes it easier to categorize the material and to decide what is most useful for your purposes. It is also important to take note of when a critical essay was written, there is no point in reading only nineteenth-century criticism (unless your essay happens to be *on* nineteenth-century criticism of the play) when much has been written since. In general, the most reliable and most sophisticated essays are to be found in books published by reputable academic publishers and in scholarly journals. Check to see if the essay you have located suits this description. Try to find other works by the same critic to get a sense of his or her reputation and expertise. Read the essay itself carefully to see if the argument is convincing and the evidence used well. The best place to look for essays would be in your university library's computerized catalogue and databases. Some of these databases can include thousands of essays on *The Tempest* alone and you need to be able to locate exactly what you want. This is where using specific search terms become necessary. If you simply type in '*Shakespeare – Tempest*', you will get more material than you can handle; instead, choose your search terms keeping your topic in mind. If you are writing on magic in the play, you could try a combination of search terms: *Tempest – Magic*, *Tempest – Alchemy* and *Tempest – Witchcraft*. If you are writing on Miranda, you could search for *Tempest – Miranda*, *Tempest – Women* or even *Tempest – Patriarchy*. You could also widen the net a bit and search for *Shakespeare – Romances – Women* or *Shakespeare-Heroines*. While the advantage of using specific and well-chosen search terms is obvious, it is sometimes useful and interesting to browse the titles that a simple search for '*The Tempest*' brings up. Even better, you could go to the section where books on Shakespeare are shelved and browse. Sometimes this 'old-fashioned' way of searching for material is the most satisfying and leads to unexpected and delightful discoveries.

Very often we assume that 'research' means searching for material on the internet. It would be relatively easy to search for critical work on *The Tempest* using any internet search engine, but you don't want to rely on the links the search engine calls up. These are likely to be student papers and other sources whose credibility and authority can be easily questioned. Unlike a library's catalogue and databases, the material on the internet has often neither been evaluated for its quality or even accuracy, nor is it organized and catalogued, and you will find that you have to sift through vast quantities of material of questionable quality to find a few gems. While it is not a good idea to look for criticism of the play online, the internet is useful for other kinds of research. There are a few good websites on Shakespeare (see the Further Reading list) and you can also find digital versions of the play or even all of Shakespeare's work. Some of these (search for '*Shakespeare Concordance*') will give you the information on how often and where certain words or phrases occur in a play, or even in the entire body of Shakespeare's work. For example, Caliban is described as a 'savage and deformed slave' in the cast of characters. You might want to find out how often the word 'slave' is used in this or in other plays by Shakespeare to get a sense of what exactly the word means to the author. The internet will let you search quickly and accurately and can yield interesting results. You can also view and compare multiple editions of the play (especially older ones, including the folios) online. The internet is also useful to listen to audio recordings of the play, find images of paintings based on *The Tempest* or look up stills or video clips from films or stage scenes. This is a very good starting point for research on *The Tempest* on stage and screen. You might also find online articles in non-academic magazines and newspapers that might give you an understanding of the cultural value of Shakespeare in the modern world. Generally speaking, the internet is a good place from which to launch one's research, and it might give you ideas on what to look for in your library. We are not yet at a point where it can be our exclusive or primary source. As discussed earlier, it can however be used in innovative ways to execute some interesting writing exercises on the play.

Why do you need to read critical works before you write your own essay on *The Tempest*? You turn to critics to gain fresh perspectives into the play and to understand it better. In your own essay, you need to explain how your own argument relates to the critical essays you have been reading. How is it similar? More importantly, how is it different? And how does it expand upon or complicate what a critic has to say? It is crucial, however, not to consider a scholarly opinion as evidence to back up a point you are making. For example, here is a student writing on Miranda:

> Miranda has no female community. As critic Ania Loomba writes, 'Miranda is the most solitary of Renaissance women protagonists, and moves on an exclusively male stage'.

This is problematic if the student fails to follow up the quote from the critic with examples from the play itself. Your evidence needs to be primarily textual. A critic is only expressing an opinion (well argued though it might be) and just because a critic says so doesn't automatically make the point you are making correct. You should also make sure that you don't quote from critics so often and at such great length that your critical essay becomes a collage of quotations from critical works. As always, the play is the focus of your essay, and whoever is reading and evaluating your essay is primarily interested in knowing what *you* (rather than another critic) have to say about *The Tempest*. Of course, it is always necessary to give critical sources credit for ideas and language that you might use in your paper.

## *Writing*

While every writer's style differs, critical essays are sometimes in danger of sounding identical to each other and it is important that writers develop their own style, as much as literary artists do. However, developing a unique writing style is different from simply 'sounding natural' or 'like yourself'. As in the case of any writing, you need to keep the purpose and audience in mind and should try not to use informalities and colloquialisms. At the same time, try to work towards a style that is not pompous and inflated. It is always a good idea to avoid overly long dense sentences and to use words you know and fully understand the meaning of. A misplaced word might make you give away your ignorance rather than impress the reader. Clarity and a neat structure are also crucial to writing a critical essay.

Begin with a title. Look at the following titles for an essay on Miranda:

- 'The Tempest'

  (Here, the writer is simply using the title of the play. This is obviously an inaccurate representation of the critical essay, which is not the same as the play).

- 'Miranda in *The Tempest*'

  (This gives the reader a sense of your topic, but is still too broad).

- 'The Miranda Trap – Racism and Sexism in *The Tempest*'

  (This title to an essay on Miranda by the critic Lori Leininger gives the reader a good idea of what the writer will explore in the essay).

Of course, a very good title is also striking. Note some of these brilliant titles given to critical essays on *The Tempest* – 'Learning to Curse: Aspects of Linguistic Colonialism in the Sixteenth Century', 'Irish Memories in *The Tempest*' and '"Knowing I loved my books": Reading *The Tempest* Intertextually'.

After the title, the introduction is what your readers will see first. The introduction to the essay is important to get readers interested and to orient them towards your argument. An arresting opening sentence is good, but very often students are tempted to begin with a 'grand' statement such as 'Shakespeare is the world's greatest writer' or even 'Life is an interesting and unexpected blend of comedy and tragedy'. Apart from being sweeping generalizations, statements like these really take the essay nowhere – avoid them. You need to get to the heart of the essay right away. Indicate which text you are writing about and make your topic very clear. Include a brief discussion leading to your argument and then state your argument. It is a good idea to indicate too that you are aware that objections can be raised to your argument and you will deal with these objections in the paper. So, for example, if you are arguing that Miranda is an assertive character in the play, you could add a sentence that goes something like:

> While it could certainly be argued that Miranda is the typical submissive daughter of Renaissance literature, a careful examination of the play indicates that she is a confident young woman and articulates her needs and desires through the play.

It is also important that the introduction (which need not be just one short paragraph) answers what is known as the 'so what question'. You might be arguing that Miranda is an assertive woman, but so what? Your introduction should also briefly explain what is significant about your argument, something you will return to at greater length when you write your paper's conclusion.

The rest of the paper should be devoted to proving your argument. This is where you will incorporate textual and historical evidence and use the critical reading you have completed. Never lose sight of your argument as you go ahead with writing and make sure that every paragraph has a point that is clear to the reader and that every paragraph advances and furthers your argument. It is also important not to jam evidence together. Deal with one piece of evidence at a time.

For example, let's assume you are still with the Miranda paper and have decided to use her 'Abhorr'd slave' speech to Caliban (1.2.352–363) as textual evidence. Don't abruptly throw in the speech. Place it in context and frame the quotation with an introductory phrase (e.g. 'Miranda's address to Caliban in the opening act is telling.'). Quote sections of the speech and follow it up with your commentary and analysis. You could discuss the editorial debate on whether these are her lines at all, close read the lines – look at the figures of speech she uses, the words she uses to describe Caliban, comment on whether her style of speech is different from Prospero's. Comment on the speech, make it clear how it furthers your argument and then move on to the next piece of evidence providing a clear transition from one piece of the discussion to the next.

As stated earlier, plot summary does not constitute evidence, nor does a quote from a critic effectively prove an argument. Also, avoid drawing evidence from your personal experience or from your observations of life (so a sentence such as 'We all know that adolescent daughters feel the need to break away from their parents' does little for your argument on Miranda). It is also usually a good idea to avoid speculating on Shakespeare's intention when writing the play (a sentence like 'It is clear that Shakespeare admired strong women, and when he wrote the play, he fully meant Miranda to be a character we can celebrate' is quite misplaced).

Your paper needs a conclusion that will emerge from what you have been saying throughout. It is important to neither simply reiterate the introduction, nor should you make new points or introduce new evidence at this stage in your essay. The conclusion is, in fact, best used to further explore the answer to the 'so what' question. Explain in detail how your argument is significant to understanding the play as a whole, how it might alter the interpretation of the play, how it contributes to current critical debates and how it might even open up further avenues for exploration.

A good critical essay not only answers many questions but also provokes readers to ask fresh ones. Responding to *The*

*Tempest* critically can be a stimulating and enjoyable exercise in thinking and writing. You can get much out of it. The play itself is an extraordinarily brilliant piece of literature. It combines poetry, philosophy and politics, the historical and the fantastic, the humorous and the profound in ways that very few literary works have succeeded in doing, and offers seemingly endless pleasure and a remarkably wide range of interpretative possibilities. *The Tempest* continues to inspire readers, critics, directors and audiences as much as it did that 'Hallowmas Nyght' in November 1611 when there was 'presented att Whithall before the kings Majestie a play Called the Tempest'.

# FURTHER READING

## Primary sources

Jourdain
Sylvester Jourdain, *A Discovery of the Barmudas, Otherwise Called the Ile of Divels* (London, 1610)

Mirandola
Giovanni Pico Della Mirandola, *Oration on the Dignity of Man* (Indianapolis, IN, 1998)

Montaigne
Michel de Montaigne, *The Complete Essays of Montaigne* (Stanford, CA, 1958)

Ovid
Publius Ovidius Naso, *The XV Books of Ovidius Naso Entytled Metamorphosis*, trans. Arthur Golding (London, 1567)

Puttenham
George Puttenham, *The Arte of English Poesie* (Cambridge, UK, and New York, 1970)

Shakespeare
William Shakespeare, *The Tempest*, ed. Virginia Mason Vaughan and Alden Vaughan, Arden Shakespeare (London, 1999)

Sidney
Philip Sidney, *A Defense of Poetry* (Oxford, UK, 1971)

Strachey
William Strachey, 'A True Repertory of the Wrack and Redemption of Sir Thomas Gates, Knight upon and from the Islands of the Bermudas', in Samuel Purchas, *Hakluytes Posthmus or Purchas His Pilgrimes*, 1625 (reprinted in Arden 3), 288–302

# Secondary sources

## *Essay collections*

Hulme and Sherman
*'The Tempest' and Its Travels*, ed. Peter Hulme and William H. Sherman (Philadelphia, PA, 2000)

Murphy
*The Tempest: Critical Essays*, ed. Patrick Murphy (New York, 2001)

Palmer
*The Tempest – A Selection of Critical Essays*, ed. D. J. Palmer (Basingstoke, 1991)

Vaughan, Critical Essays
*Critical Essays on Shakespeare's 'The Tempest'*, ed. Virginia Mason and Alden T. Vaughan (New York and London, 1998)

Vaughan, 'Introduction'
'Introduction', *The Tempest*, ed. Virginia Mason Vaughan and Alden Vaughan, Arden Shakespeare (London, 1999), 1–138

White
*The Tempest : Contemporary Critical Essays*, ed. R. S. White (London, 1999)

## *Other sources*

Addison
Joseph Addison, *The Spectator*, ed. Donald F Bond, Vol. 2 (Oxford, UK, 1965)

Bakhtin, 'Discourse'
M. M. Bakhtin, 'Discourse in the Novel', in *Literary Theory: An Anthology*, ed. Julie Rivkin and Michael Ryan (Malden, MA, 2004), 674–85

Bakhtin, *Speech Genres*
M. M. Bakhtin, *Speech Genres and Other Late Essays*, trans. Vern W. McGee, ed. C. Emerson and M. Holquist (Austin, TX, 1986)

**Barker and Hulme**

Francis Barker and Peter Hulme, ' "Nymphs and Reapers Heavily Vanish": The Discursive Con-Texts of The Tempest', in *Alternative Shakespeares* (London, 2002), 195–209

**Bate**

Jonathan Bate, *Shakespeare and Ovid* (Oxford, UK, 1993)

**Berger**

Harry Berger, 'Miraculous Harp: A Reading of Shakespeare's Tempest', *SSt 5* (1969), 253–83

**Brooks**

Cleanth Brooks, 'The Language of Paradox', in *Literary Theory: An Anthology*, ed. Julie Rivkin and Michael Ryan (Malden, MA, 2004), 28–39

**Brotton, 'Carthage'**

Jerry Brotton, 'Carthage and Tunis, *The Tempest* and Tapestries', in *The Tempest and Its Travels*, ed. Peter Hulme and William Sherman (Philadelphia, PA, 2000), 132–7

**Brotton, 'This Tunis'**

Jerry Brotton, '"This Tunis, Sir, Was Carthage": Contesting Colonialism in *The Tempest*', in *Post-Colonial Shakespeares*, ed. Ania Loomba and Martin Orkin (London, 1998), 23–42

**Brower**

Reuben Brower, *The Fields of Light: An Experiment in Critical Reading* (Oxford, UK, 1951)

**Brown**

Paul Brown, ' "This Thing of Darkness I Acknowledge Mine" *The Tempest* and the Discourse of Colonialism', in *Political Shakespeare: New Essays in Cultural Materialism*, ed. Jonathan Dollimoe and Alan Sinfield (Manchester, 1985), 48–71

**Callaghan**

Dympna Callaghan, 'Irish Memories in *The Tempest*', in *Shakespeare without Women* (London, 2000), 97–138

**Coleridge**

Samuel Taylor Coleridge, *Coleridge on Shakespeare – Text of the Lectures, 1811–12*, ed. R. A. Foakes (Charlottsville, VA, 1971)

Danson
Lawrence Danson, *Shakespeare's Dramatic Genres* (Oxford, UK and New York, 2000)

Dobson
Michael Dobson, '"Remember/First to Possess His Books": The Appropriation of *The Tempest*', 1700–1800', *SS* 43 (1991), 99–107

Dowden
Edward Dowden, *Shakespeare: A Critical Study of His Mind and Art* (New York, 1899)

Dryden
John Dryden, *Of Dramatic Poesy and Other Critical Essays*, ed. George Watson, Vol. 1 (London, 1962)

Eagleton
Terry Eagleton, *How to Read a Poem* (Malden, MA, 2007)

Eliot
T. S. Eliot, *The Sacred Wood and Major Early Essays* (Mineola, NY, 1997)

Fiedler
Leslie A. Fiedler, *The Stranger in Shakespeare* (New York, 1972)

Foucault
M. Foucault, *The Archeology of Knowledge* (New York, 1982)

Fuchs
Barbara Fuchs, 'Conquering Islands: Contextualizing *The Tempest*', *SQ* 48.1 (1997), 45–62

Gillies
John Gillies, 'The Figure of the New World in *The Tempest*', in *'The Tempest' and Its Travels*, ed. Peter Hulme and William Sherman, (Philadelphia, PA, 2000), 180–200

Greenblatt, 'Learning'
Stephen Greenblatt, 'Learning to Curse: Aspects of Linguistic Colonialism in the Sixteenth Century', in *Learning to Curse: Essays in Early Modern Culture* (New York and London, 1992), 16–39

Greenblatt, *Marvelous*
Stephen Greenblatt, *Marvelous Possessions: The Wonder of the New World* (Chicago, 1991)

Greenblatt, *Shakespearean*
Stephen Greenblatt, *Shakespearean Negotiations: The Circulation of Social Energy in Renaissance England* (Berkeley, CA, 1988)

Greenblatt, 'Tempest'
Stephen Greenblatt, '*The Tempest*: Martial Law in the Land of Cockaigne', in *Shakespeare: The Last Plays*, ed. Ryan Kierna (London, 1999), 206–44

Griffiths
Trevor R. Griffiths, '"This Island's Mine": Caliban and Colonialism', *Yearbook of English Studies* 13 (1983), 159–80

Gurr
Andrew Gurr, 'The Tempest's Tempest at Blackfriars', *SS* 41 (1989), 91–102

Hall
Kim F. Hall, *Things of Darkness: Economies of Race and Gender in Early Modern England* (Ithaca, NY, 1995)

Hawkes
Terence Hawkes, 'Swisser-Swatter: Making a Man of English Letters', in *Alternative Shakespeares* (London, 2002), 26–47

Hendricks and Parker
Margo Hendricks and Patricia Parker, *Women, 'Race,' and Writing in the Early Modern Period* (London, Routledge, 1994)

Hulme, 'Hurricane'
Peter Hulme, 'Hurricane in the Caribees: The Constitution of the Discourse of English Colonialism', in *1642: Literature and Power in the Seventeenth Century*, ed. Francis Barker (Colchester, 1981), 55–83

Hulme, 'Prospero'
Peter Hulme, 'Prospero and Caliban', in his *Colonial Encounters: Europe and the Native Caribbean, 1492–1797* (London, 1986), 89–134

Iser
Wolfgang Iser, 'The Reading Process: A Phenomenological Approach', *New Literary History* 3.2 (1972), 279–99

James
Henry James, 'Introduction to *The Tempest*', in *The Complete Works of William Shakespeare*, ed. Sidney Lee (New York, 1907), 16: ix–xxxii

Jameson

Anna Jameson, *Shakespeare's Heroines* (London, 1832, reprint Gramercy, 2003)

Johnson

Samuel Johnson, *The Works of William Shakespeare* (London, 1766)

Kahn

Coppelia Kahn, 'The Providential Tempest and the Shakespearean Family', in *Representing Shakespeare: New Psychoanalytic Essays*, ed. Murray Schwartz (Baltimore, MD, 1980), 217–43

Kastan

David Scott Kastan, '"The Duke of Milan/and His Brave Son": Old Histories and New in *The Tempest*', in *New Casebooks: Shakespeare's Romances*, ed. Alison Thorne (Basingstoke, UK, 2003), 226–44

Kermode

Frank Kermode, 'Introduction', *The Tempest*, The Arden Shakespeare (London, 1954; rev. edn, 1961), xi–xciii

Knapp

Jeffrey Dana Knapp, *An Empire Nowhere: England and America, from 'Utopia' to 'The Tempest'* (Berkeley, CA, 1989)

Knight

Wilson Knight, *The Crown of Life* (Oxford, UK, 1947)

Lamb

Charles Lamb, 'On the Tragedies of Shakespeare; with Reference to Their Fitness for Stage-Representation', in *Selected Writings*, ed. J. E. Morpurgo (New York, 2003), 241–59

Lee

Sidney Lee, *A Life of William Shakespeare* (London, 1989)

Lindley

David Lindley, 'Music, Masque and Meaning in *The Tempest*', in *The Court Masque*, ed. David Lindley (Manchester, 1984), 47–59

Loomba

Ania Loomba, 'Seizing the Book', in *Gender, Race, Renaissance Drama* (New York, 1992), 142–58

Lotman

Yury Lotman, *Analysis of the Poetic Text* (Ann Arbor, MI, 1976)

Lupton
Julia Reinhard Lupton, 'Creature Caliban', *SQ* 51.1 (2000), 1–23

Malone
Edmond Malone, *An Account of the Incidents, from Which the Title and Part of the Story of Shakespeare's Tempest Were Derived; and Its True Date Ascertained* (London, 1808)

Marcus
Leah S. Marcus, 'The Blue-Eyed Witch', in *Unediting the Renaissance: Shakespeare, Marlowe, Milton* (London, 1996), 5–17

McDonald, 'Reading'
Russ McDonald, 'Reading *The Tempest*', *SS* 43 (1991), 15–28

McDonald, *Shakespeare's*
Russ McDonald, *Shakespeare's Late Style* (Cambridge, UK and New York, 2006)

Mebane
John S. Mebane, *Renaissance Magic and the Return of the Golden Age: The Occult Tradition and Marlowe, Jonson, and Shakespeare* (Lincoln, NE, 1989)

Mowat
Barbara A. Mowat, 'Prospero, Agrippa, and Hocus Pocus', *English Literary Renaissance* 11.3 (1981), 281–303

Murphy
Andrew Murphy, 'The Transmission of Shakespeare's texts', in *The New Cambridge Companion to Shakespeare*, ed. Margreta De Grazia and Stanley Wells (Cambridge, UK and New York, 2010), 61–76

Orgel, 'Introduction'
Stephen Orgel, 'Introduction', *The Tempest* by William Shakespeare (Oxford, UK and New York, 1987), 1–87

Orgel, 'Prospero's'
Stephen Orgel, 'Prospero's Wife', *Representations* 8 (1984), 1–13

Pettegree
Andrew Pettegree, *The Book in the Renaissance* (New Haven, CT, 2010)

Singh

Jyotsna G. Singh, 'Caliban versus Miranda: Race and Gender Conflicts in Postcolonial Rewritings of The Tempest', in *Feminist Readings of Early Modern Culture: Emerging Subjects* (Cambridge, UK, 1996), 191–209

Shklovsky

Viktor Shklovsky, 'Art as Technique', in *Literary Theory: An Anthology*, ed. Julie Rivkin and Michael Ryan (Malden, MA, 2004), 15–21

Skura

Meredith Anne Skura, 'Discourse and the Individual: The Case of Colonialism in *The Tempest*', *SQ* 40.1 (1989), 42–69

SQ

*Shakespeare Quarterly*

SS

*Shakespeare Survey*

SSt

*Shakespeare Studies*

Strachey

Lytton Strachey, 'Shakespeare's Final period', in his *Literary Essays* (San Diego, 1969), 1–16

Thompson

Ann Thompson, '"Miranda, Where's Your Sister?": Reading Shakespeare's *The Tempest*', in *Feminist Criticism: Theory and Practice*, ed. Susan Sellers (Toronto, 1991), 45–55

Vaughan, A. T.

Alden T. Vaughan, 'Shakespeare's Indian: The Americanization of Caliban', *SQ* 39.2 (1988), 137–53

Vaughan, V. M.

Virginia Mason Vaughan, 'Literary Invocations of *The Tempest*', in *Cambridge Companion to Shakespeare's Last Plays*, ed. Catherine M. S. Alexander (Cambridge, UK and New York, 2009), 155–72

Vaughan and Vaughan

Alden T. Vaughan and Virginia Mason Vaughan, *Shakespeare's Caliban: A Cultural History* (Cambridge, UK, 1993)

Warner

Marina Warner, '"The Foul Witch" and Her "Freckled Whelp":
Circean Mutations in the New World', in *'The Tempest' and Its
Travels*, ed. Peter Hulme and William Sherman (Philadelphia,
PA, 2000), 97–113

Wells

Stanley Wells, 'Shakespeare's Comedies', in *The New Cambridge
Companion to Shakespeare*, ed. Margreta de Grazia and
Stanley Wells (Cambridge, UK, and New York, 2010), 105–20

Willis

Deborah Willis, 'Shakespeare's *Tempest* and the Discourse of
Colonialism', *SEL: Studies in English Literature, 1500–1900*
29.2 (1989), 277–89

Wilson

Daniel Wilson, *Caliban: The Missing Link* (London, Macmillan, 1873)

Yates

Frances A. Yates, 'Prospero: The Shakespearean Magus', in her
*The Occult Philosophy in the Elizabethan Age* (London, 1979),
159–63

## *Appropriations of* The Tempest

Auden

W. H. Auden, *Collected Poems*, ed. Edward Mendelson (New
York, 1976)

Brathwaite

Kamau Brathwaite, *The Arrivants: A New World Trilogy* (Oxford,
UK, 1969)

Browning

Robert Browning, 'Caliban upon Setebos; or, Natural Theology in
the Island', in *The Poetical Works of Robert Browning*, Vol. 7
(London, 1889), 149–61

Césaire

Aimé Césaire, *A Tempest*, trans. Richard Miller (New York, 1993)

Dryden

John Dryden and William Davenant, *The Tempest : Or, The Enchanted Island* (London, 1670), reprinted in George R. Guffey, *After the Tempest* (Los Angeles, 1969)

Hilda Doolittle (H. D.)

Hilda Doolittle (H. D.), *By Avon River* (New York, 1949)

Johnson

Lemuel Johnson, *Highlife for Caliban* (Ann Arbor, MI, 1973)

Lamming

George Lamming, 'A Monster, a Child, a Slave', in his *Pleasures of Exile* (London, 1984), 95–117

MacKaye

Percy MacKaye, *Caliban by the Yellow Sands* (Garden City, NY, 1916)

Mannoni

O. Mannoni, *Prospero and Caliban: The Psychology of Colonization*, 2nd edition, trans. Pamela Powesland (New York, 1964)

Namjoshi

Suniti Namjoshi, 'Snapshots of Caliban', *Because of India: Selected Poems and Fables* (London, 1989), 85–102

Renan

Ernest Renan, *Caliban: A Philosophical Drama Continuing 'The Tempest' of William Shakespeare*, trans. Eleanor Grant Vickery (New York, The Shakespeare Press, 1896)

Retamar

Roberto Fernandez Retamar, 'Caliban: Notes toward a Discussion of Culture in Our America', *The Massachusetts Review* 15 (1974), 11–16

Rodó

José Enrique Rodó, *Ariel*, trans. F. J. Stimson (Boston, 1922)

Warner

Marina Warner, *Indigo* (New York, 1992)

# Internet sources

http://shakespeare.mit.edu/
A searchable site with digitized complete works of Shakespeare.

http://shakespeare.palomar.edu/
This website named 'Mr. William Shakespeare and the Internet' attempts to serve as 'an annotated guide to the scholarly Shakespeare resources available on the internet'. It has a wealth of material and is worth exploring in detail. It includes a fairly extensive biographical information, background on Elizabethan theatre, reviews of books on Shakespeare and his works, criticism of individual plays, including *The Tempest*, and a small selection of primary texts. It also provides links to other sites, including editions of the plays, Shakespeare festivals and study guides.

www.folger.edu/index.cfm
The Folger Shakespeare Library (Washington, DC) website has valuable resources for teachers and students including lesson plans, study guides and an online discussion forum to exchange ideas on teaching and studying the plays.

www.opensourceshakespeare.org/
This website labels itself an 'experiment in literary technology' and is among the best 'concordances' available. You can read the entire play online and use the search function to search for words and phrases in the play and across the entire body of Shakespeare's work.

www.rarebookroom.org/Control/shaf1b1/index.html
This site has a facsimile version of the First Folio. There are several other sites that will let you look at and read the First Folio and other early editions of *The Tempest*, both in facsimile version and as transcriptions of the original. Many of these sites are linked off the palomar.edu site listed above.

www.speak-the-speech.com/thetempestpage.htm
This website allows you to listen to a good reading of *The Tempest* produced by a professional, non-profit audio theatre company called Speak the Speech.